THE HEROES HAVE GONE

Personal Essays on Sport, Popular Culture, and the American West

by

JIM W. CORDER

illustrations by
the author

Edited, with an Afterword

by

JAMES S. BAUMLIN
Missouri State University
and

KEITH D. MILLER
Arizona State University

QVI·SCIT·PERDIT

MISSOVRI

Copyright © 2008 Moon City Press.
Moon City is a press imprint of the Department of English,
Missouri State University, Springfield MO 65897.
For email queries, contact <jbaumlin@missouristate.edu>.

Library of Congress Cataloging-in-Publication Data

Corder, Jim W. (Jim Wayne), 1929–
The heroes have gone : personal essays on the American West, sport,
and popular culture / by Jim W. Corder ; edited, with a
preface by James S. Baumlin and Keith D. Miller.
p. cm.

ISBN: 978-0-913785-11-9 (pbk.)

1. Corder, Jim W. (Jim Wayne), 1929–Anecdotes. 2. Corder, Jim W.
(Jim Wayne), 1929–Childhood and youth–Anecdotes.
3. Jayton (Tex.)–Biography–Anecdotes. 4. Jayton (Tex.)–Social life
and customs–Anecdotes. 5. West (U.S.)–Social life and
customs–Anecdotes. 6. Sports–United States–Anecdotes. 7. Popular
culture–United States–Anecdotes. 8. Authors,
American–20th century–Biography–Anecdotes. 9. American poetry.
I. Baumlin, James S. II. Miller, Keith D. III. Title.

CT275.C7813A3 2008
978'.034–dc22
2007047781

The Heroes Have Gone
Table of Contents

The Glove

I didn't know then that it was enchantment. A fellow doesn't know much about that sort of thing in the second grade, or about incantations and charms, or about whatever might thrill or bewitch or enrapture. But for the glory that came around me and in me when I looked at it, held it, and put it on, I had as well put on the armor of the Lord or the shining gear of Galahad. I didn't know, either, that one day the enchantment would end.

Later, I would reckon that the enchantment had already begun, but it was the arrival of the sign and token, my ball glove, that lets me set some date as beginning time. I was already playing ball pretty often, I'd guess, else there'd have been no occasion for the glove I got for Christmas in 1937. I got nothing else that Christmas, and that was no matter: the glove was plenty. Years later, when we chanced to talk about it, my mother told me that in 1937 in West Texas, one present was all there could be. I wish I had known or thought to tell her, "Yes ma'am, indeed, the glove was all there could be."

My brother got a glove that Christmas, too. Our gloves were not identical, though I was certainly willing to agree that his, too, was beautiful. He was already five years older than I, and I have never caught up with him, and it has taken me most of these years since to catch on that the glove was probably his first, too. Now, I wonder what he thought and felt. Then, and in many of the intervening years, I expect that I didn't wonder what he thought and felt. Perhaps I didn't suspect that he was a real person over there, doing his own thinking and feeling. Perhaps I had already caught and held him, trapped him in my conception of him as brother. Probably I have often, if not always, done so since. Now I wonder what he thought and felt when our gloves came.

But of course he was older and given to more sophisticated ways. He may have already known what I needed another couple of Christmases to figure out—how our parents got the gloves, how the gloves came to us. Such things weren't available in Jayton, the little town where we lived, population about 650. Places to shop weren't abundant there; those that existed had scant room for anything but necessities. Huls' Drug Store was by the movie house just off the square. Jones' Drug Store was on the north side of the square. Neither had ball gloves. Alongside Jones' Drug Store was Bryant-Link Dry Goods, the nearest there was to a general merchandise store. You could

get clothes there, and shoes, and thread and material, and other stuff that kids didn't think about much. Robinson's over on the east side of the square had groceries and hardware and some dry goods and, somewhere in the back, a dark and dangerous place where they took care of dead bodies, fixing folks for burial. Robinson's thus was able to advertise, "Everything From the Cradle to the Grave." A Chevrolet dealer was on the south side of the square, along with the local office of West Texas Utilities. On the west side were the offices of *The Jayton Chronicle* (the weekly newspaper), the Barefoot Hotel, and the bank. The post office was behind the bank, and Gardner's Grocery was at the northwest corner of the square. You didn't have to set aside a whole day to do your shopping in Jayton, unless you really intended to linger a long time over each item.

But on Christmas in 1937, I didn't pause to wonder where the glove came from. I may have supposed that since the glove itself was magic, and since getting a glove was magic, then the source for gloves was probably magic, too.

Later, I learned, or maybe my brother told me, that our gloves came from Montgomery Ward, which, of course, was wonderfully elsewhere, though I had no notion of where that might be. In time, I learned that my mother made her one-yearly order late in the summer, when the new Montgomery Ward catalog came out. That's how my father, my brother, and I got most of what we wore. My mother made most of her own clothes. Each year, she apparently found a way to add to her order a Christmas present for my brother and one for me. We never actually caught her doing this, and we never actually caught her hiding anything when the package came from Montgomery Ward, but that's where our gloves came from.

The little house we lived in that Christmas in 1937 was the last house to the north in Jayton. It had three rooms, two across the front, one—the kitchen—in back to make a T. The bathroom facilities included a bucket, a dipper, and a wash basin that sat on a stand outside the kitchen door and an outhouse some thirty or forty yards down the path. The exterior of the house was unpainted board and batten. By the 1960s, the house was being used for hay storage. Now, it is gone. Then, it sat right on the first edge of the badly-eroded territory known as the Croton Breaks. The Breaks make a rough rectangle, some thirty to forty miles from here to there, cornered by Jayton on the southwest, Aspermont on the southeast, Guthrie on the northeast, and Dickens on the northwest. I didn't know then that the territory had a name—to me, it was just The Canyons.

We went out into The Canyons—my mother, my father, my brother, and I, my father carrying his axe—one Sunday afternoon before Christmas, hunting the right cedar tree to use for our Christmas tree. I remember only moments of the expedition, particularly my father dragging the tree behind him as we headed home. In later years, I heard him recall the day more than once. "We looked all over for just the right tree," he'd say, and then, "You know, had to be shaped just so, she thought, and big enough to suit her." Then he'd say, "It was so big, I had to chop it off four times before we could get it in the front door." Then my mother would say, "Well, it needed to be a big tree. I knew there wasn't going to be much under it."

My father set it up somehow, and my mother decorated it. I cannot call the decorations back to mind. She needn't have worried about how little would be under the tree. On Christmas morning, the ball gloves were there.

My brother's glove was of a dark leather, mine of a light. The leather was soft and unshaped, so that the glove lay mostly limp and flat. Crossed leather laces connected the thumb with the index finger, but the other fingers were unconnected. That was all right and as it should be; that's what gloves mostly looked like then. I claim no expertise in the matter of ball gloves, but when I look at the old catalogs in the library, I'm led to conclude that my glove (and my brother's) was a relatively early specimen of the Middle Period in baseball glove design. From the time of their early use until, in some instances, just about up to the 1920s, gloves were thin and scarcely larger than the hand. I have not, however, actually seen early gloves, and so must reckon only on the evidence of photographs, sometimes dimly seen. Beginning, I'd guess in the late teens or early 20s, they are larger, both a little longer and considerably wider, with thickly padded thumbs and little fingers to help in forming a pocket. My glove was of such a design, and a picture of Giants pitcher, Carl Hubbell, made in 1929, shows him wearing a glove that looks pretty much like my brother's glove, only bigger. In the course of this middle period, manufacturers began to pad the heel of the gloves more, giving more shape to a pocket for the ball, and they began to lace all the fingers together, to prevent a certain splaying that would occur if a fellow depended too much on the glove instead of on his hands. In the Recent Period, beginning, I'd guess, in the early 1960s, manufacturers began using a firmer, thicker leather and learned how to shape the gloves, mostly much bigger now, into the formidable scoops of today. They look sort of like they would go ahead and catch the ball for you, unassisted, if you would just get them in the vicinity of the right place.

The Sears, Roebuck and Company's Fall and Winter, 1928–1929, catalog has a nice half-page display of ball gloves. I haven't found early Montgomery Ward catalogs, but I hope to. It may be that they are much scarcer than the Sears Roebuck catalog—many people, I'm given to understand, preferred the quality of paper in the Montgomery Ward catalogs for their final uses. I suppose it's possible that all potential archival copies may have disappeared gradually in the outhouses of America. At any rate, the Sears Roebuck catalog shows four catcher's mitts and two first baseman's mitts, all entirely too esoteric for my taste. The catalog shows six fielder's gloves, priced at $1.37, $1.75, $1.98, $2.69, $2.98, and, the priciest model, signed by Grover Cleveland Alexander, at $3.87. Below them is a display of boys' gloves: one catcher's mitt and two fielder's gloves—one priced at 59 cents, the other at 79 cents. They look pretty much like the gloves my brother and I got. The display in the 1946–1947 catalog is sparser—I guess materials were still not easily available so soon after the end of World War II. The catalog shows only two fielder's gloves, one at $3.77, the other at $4.89. They, too, look pretty much like the gloves we got, though they appear to be padded better, and the costlier one has a nicer net of wide straps between thumb and index finger.

The Sears Roebuck Fall and Winter catalog for 1936–1937—as close as I can get to the right years, if not the right company—is sparse, too. Those weren't fat years. One catcher's mitt appears, one first baseman's mitt, and three fielder's gloves, priced at $1.49, $1.95, and $3.29. The cheapest model looks a lot like my glove, the middle glove a lot like my brother's. I hope that's the way it was. I hope to God they paid more for his than for mine—he waited longer.

But I'm looking at Sears Roebuck models, and I'm not altogether sure that I can trust them. I don't have to, now, though I still can't be sure about what my brother's glove looked like. I have known all along in my memory that mine wasn't much of a glove, but it was the most beautiful thing I had ever seen. I used it for years, until I was in high school. You could make yourself believe that you'd get a good pocket in it if you pounded it with your other hand a lot, which I did. Some favored tying the glove around a ball when it wasn't in use, so that it would take the shape just so, and I tried that, too, but I never favored the more extreme procedure of wetting the glove down and then tying it around a ball.

Pocket or not, it was the most beautiful thing I had ever seen. And I haven't entirely forgotten, either, the warm, delicious sense of waking the next morning, lying there for a moment, knowing that the glove was still there. I never expected a ball glove.

In time, I came to treat the glove as an ordinary thing. Once, I forgot it and left it lying overnight on the front porch. The next morning, it was in the front yard. The small dog that lived with us had chewed on it some and scuffed it around, teething and playing. I cannot forget now—and I don't believe that I have exaggerated—the sickness that swept through me that morning: in the moments when I stood and looked at it lying there torn in the yard, and in the longer moments when I sat or walked down in The Canyons, carrying it with me, I knew that there wouldn't be another glove, not that year, perhaps not the next. Indeed, as far as I could tell then, there would never be another glove.

As it happened, I was able to stuff and sew and salvage my glove, and I used it for years. I put it down finally, I supposed, when I got a new glove while I was in high school. I guess I didn't think about it any more.

Then, one day, we were visiting my parents, not long before their deaths in 1988. My mother remembered something she had for me and left the room. We heard her. I believe she was rooting around in her closet. After a while, she came back and handed me my ball glove.

I had known in my memory that it wasn't much of a glove, and now I could see for myself. No matter: it was beautiful. It lies close by my desk now, and it is still beautiful.

I won't ever know exactly why she kept it. Perhaps she knew how much it had mattered to me. Perhaps she thought I would remember.

The Game Was There Before I Was

Probably it was in the summer or early fall of 1939—sometime close to the beginning of the second grade—that I began to find out about playing ball. Charley Gehringer, I know, was already the established second baseman for the Detroit Tigers. I would learn later that he had been for some time; I would also learn that some sports writers called him "The Mechanical Man," others, "The Grey Ghost." Once I heard about him, I followed his career whenever I could. I loved him. I came soon to think that he was the best. I don't know how I learned about him, or when I learned about him, or what I learned about him, but I wanted to be Charley Gehringer, though I probably still wanted to be myself, too. I'm pretty sure that I'm close to the right time, too, because I know that the young rookie, Joe DiMaggio, and I came upon the scene at about the same time and rose to fame together, he in actuality, I only in my mind.

But I can't call back a magical moment or day or month when I discovered softball and baseball. I understand the difference between the two games, but in my mind they were never really different—each meant playing ball, and whenever I discovered softball and baseball, I believed then, too, in playing ball. Playing ball was exquisite joy, so exquisite that you couldn't really say anything about it, though I wouldn't have known to say that then, and I wouldn't have known to say, either, that playing ball was breath-taking, sweet, and poignant, but I believed in playing ball.

Sometimes, now, I still do. Sometimes, even now, I think that if my eyes were good, if my knees would hold out, if various other joints and sinews would take the strain, I'd still be playing, waiting for my breakthrough into the big leagues. Mostly, I don't think such things anymore, but I do sometimes suppose that, if there is a heaven, a perpetual game will be going on, and there'll always be room for you to get into the game at the position where you want to play. When I am supposing, I also like to suppose that there will be occasional breaks between innings for other pursuits, interests, and pleasures—you know, maybe a thousand years in the field, a thousand years at bat, and a thousand years for a break.

But the truth is, I don't know exactly how or when I found out about playing ball. I must have been playing, or imagining that I was playing, by the summer of 1937, though, or there'd have been no reason for a glove that Christmas.

I expect I was playing by that time, playing then and thereafter only with whatever instinctive physical abilities I may have had, playing then and thereafter without benefit of discipline or tutelage. When I ran onto a field to play, I carried with me only gladness and my glove.

And, in those first years, even the gladness wasn't always pure. Well, pure maybe, but not whole. Sometimes, I gave part of it away to football, though I would learn better.

Once, on a Friday evening in early October just after dark, I took a flight from Memphis back home to Fort Worth. Along the way, I saw lovely jewels below me and didn't realize until I had seen a couple what it was that I was seeing. It was, remember, a Friday evening. We were passing over town after town. Those pretty baubles below, green ovals set in gold, were football fields, and the Friday game was being played by high-school teams from Memphis to Fort Worth and on beyond. Seeing them called back old times, other Fridays, though there were no lights at the field in Jayton in 1938, and few planes flew overhead.

I guess it may already be plain that as I was growing up— and in my mind, that was still going on this morning—I was an ardent though inadequately motivated and insufficiently directed jock, clear through to the bone. Little came of it.

Jayton claimed some 650 souls in population. That doesn't include Mr. Boone Bilberry, who, according to the Baptists, didn't have a soul. He drank a little. I went to school in Jayton through the fourth grade. When my brother was in the ninth grade, the year before we moved to the big city, Jayton High School decided that it could field a football team. It's easy enough to reckon that a town of 650 souls, not counting Boone Bilberry, wouldn't have a large number of high-school age males, even including the boys from farms around the town. At any rate, my brother played on the team while he was in the ninth grade and again in the tenth grade until we moved away. It's what one did if one was a young male with any sense. I went and watched practice most days, and on one of the early days saw the principal drawing the yard lines off with a hoe. Once, when he reached the side near where I was standing,

he turned, squinted along the line he had drawn in the dirt, turned back to me, and said, "Well, it'd look straight to a blind man." That's the only time I ever talked to the principal.

Baseball was my true first love, but football was what a young male did in a small West Texas town. I expected to be a football player. I had some natural though untutored ability, and probably would have been a football player in that small town. But we moved to the city, and there were more folks, and some of them were a whole lot larger. By the time I was a junior in high school, I had my full height, six feet, but I weighed only 135 pounds, and I had somewhere acquired an entirely unjustified regard for the well-being of my ungainly person. I abandoned football.

That's just as well. My football career would have existed only in my mind, and besides, I was always a little ashamed of my adulterous fling with football. Still, it was significant while it lasted, not least because of events occurring the fall of 1938, in Jayton.

"Never think," Rainer Maria Rilke remarked somewhere, "that there is more in life than can be packed into childhood." What got packed into 1938 was particularly important to me. I discovered universities and the gallant lives of university athletes. I'm not sure I knew that colleges and universities existed before that time. I probably did, but they had made no great impression on me. But in 1938 my family got a radio, and quite by accident I discovered that football games were broadcast on Saturday afternoons. Listening to any one game taught me the names of universities all across the land, since broadcasters periodically announced scores from other games. I heard for the first time the music of university bands at halftime. But most of all I discovered Davey O'Brien, Ki Aldrich, Connie Sparks, and all the others on TCU's 1938 national championship team. They came to personify both university athletics and the university. I heard about them all that fall.

First they beat Centenary, and the headline on September 24 read, "O'Brien's Long Shots Down Gents, 13–10." Then they beat Arkansas, and the headline said, "Frogs' Power Outlasts Porker Passes, 21–14." Then they played Temple University, and the headline said, "Frogs Smash Owls in Second Period, 28–6." Next was A&M, and the headline said, "Frogs Smash Aggies, 34–6! Aldrich, O'Brien Star." Then it was Marquette: "Frogs Strike Quickly, Coast to 21–0 Victory." Baylor was next: "Frogs Smash Bears with Power, Passes, 39–7." Then came a simple headline, "Frogs Beat Tulsa, 21–0." The headline on Sunday, November 12, said, "O'Brien's Passes Sink Texas, 28–6." Then they played Rice, and the headline read, "Frogs' Passes Punish Owls, 29–7." Finally, the headline for Sunday, November 26, said, "Frogs Use Power to Beat Ponies, 20–7, for Conference Title."

Well, if you're about nine, expecting to be a football player, and have just discovered a winning team only some 250 miles away, it just doesn't get any better than that.

Then at Christmas I got the first book I ever owned all by myself, *Andy at Yale*, and it told about Andy and his friends at

Yale and how the lads went out for football. Just a little later, TCU played Carnegie Tech in the Sugar Bowl and won, 15–7.

It was quite a year: I learned about universities, and I learned about them in the most thrilling way—through the accounts of *Andy at Yale*, and through the deeds of Davey O'Brien and his teammates. That old feeling doesn't go away easily: "Don't think life is more than what is packed into childhood." It still comes sometimes when I see the grace of a defensive back going high into a crowd and taking away the pass they don't want him to have, or when I see a clean block that breaks a running back loose, or when I see a quarterback throw a forty-yard pass that drops right over the shoulder and into the hands of an end who's going full out down the sideline.

That old feeling doesn't go away easily, and perhaps never goes away entirely, but it fades because one learns other lessons. It fades, fades, until there's nothing left but a whisper of old time.

I seldom watch football games on television any more, and so seldom pout if the team I favor happens to lose. In 1938, I thought I was hearing and reading about athletes who not only personified the university, but who were also known and cared for by their classmates. I've learned, though, that *Andy at Yale* told about a world that may never have existed, or if it did, it has long since vanished. One doesn't simply "go out" for football much these days, and most athletes are known to the student body at large only as stereotypes and, later, as commodities. And besides, that world of *Andy at Yale* was all-white and elitist.

Nothing much turned out the way I imagined it would, and I guess I'm a little shocked, but not much surprised. Some years ago Jayton changed over to six-man football, and in the fall, 1985, won the state championship. I'm glad for the players and for the school and the town, but it isn't quite the same in my mind as that glorious game when I saw my brother go high in the air to intercept that pass.

Most things aren't quite the same. Those jewels in towns across the country are bright only once in a while, and football is not what I had somehow wanted it to be. Neither am I, for that matter. I didn't turn out to be Sammy Baugh or Davey O'Brien—or Joe DiMaggio or Charley Gehringer.

I know how and when I came to know about football. It would have happened sooner or later to a young male in a small West Texas town, but it happened to me in 1938 when we came to have a radio and when my brother played on the Jayton High School team. My football fling was a small fancy, though, not as long a love as that I've had for softball and baseball, or as deep.

And I guess I know when I began to learn about playing ball—along in 1937 before I got the glove.

But when and how and why did I begin to learn that narrative serial that has stayed so long? When and how and why did I begin to learn that rhetoric of my boyhood that has remained? When and how and why did I learn that softball and baseball took precedence in the language? If you say that you are going outside to play ball, or if you say that you were up at school play-ing a little ball, the words always indicate that you're involved with softball or baseball. If you're doing something else, you've got to say so. You play volleyball, you play football, and you play basketball, but playing ball is playing ball.

I guess I'll never know for sure just how and why playing ball took hold and took precedence. I'm pretty sure that a predi-lection for playing a little ball was not already and always pres-ent in my genetic character. I'm pretty sure that there was no specific initiation into the rites of playing ball and that there was no fixed period of indoctrination—I didn't learn how and when to scratch until years later, and I never did learn how and when and where to spit.

Still, playing ball has to be constructed into the self, learned, even if one never learns how to play well. Knowing how to play well is not a prerequisite for the love of playing ball. Either can be learned, and maybe either can be taught, but I don't know exactly where or when or how I had my education, and if I did know, the knowledge wouldn't altogether explain how playing ball came to be, not something out there, but already in here in my mind and soon, too, in the habits of my eyes and hands and arms and legs and feet.

I don't learn much from *The Jayton Chronicle*, the weekly newspaper. Perhaps I would learn more about my early indoc-trination if I could read all the issues from those days. I can't.

Earlier, I went in search of *The Jayton Chronicle* for other pur-poses. Eventually, I found microfilms of some issues. In the years I was most interested in (and am most interested in now), from 1934, or about the time I started remembering, to 1946, or about the time I graduated high school, there might have been, probably were, 676 issues, assuming 52 per year. I found 241 issues on microfilm. Of the possible issues in those years, there are 435 I do not have.

As I read *The Jayton Chronicle*, sometimes surprised by the news, by news I had not heard, by news that I remembered so surely and so mistakenly, I found myself wondering, again and again, what I would have learned, what would have startled me, what I could have seen in a new way that I had misremembered, if only I could read the missing issues.

Perhaps the mysteries of playing ball are told in the pages of the missing issues.

There are always missing issues.

I do learn from the issue of May 11, 1934, that baseball fans were asked to meet down at the Palace, the movie theater, to organize a baseball club. On May 18, Mr. Wade, the editor, writes, "Let's go, folks, because Jayton's gonna PLAY BALL!" I don't know what they played: as I grew part of the way up, people sometimes used either *baseball* or *softball* when they were talking about softball. Whatever it was they were playing, almost certainly softball, the June 1 issue reports a 7–3 victory for Jayton over Rotan. The June 8 issue reports a 13–11 win over Peacock, and the June 15 issue says that the team has beaten Peacock again. The June 22 issue says that fans and business houses are supporting the team, though Peacock has just beat Jayton, 11–2. From the July 13 issue I learn that the team has now beaten Peacock again, and also Aspermont, but the next week's issue reports a loss. I learn, too, that the team from McAdoo is coming to engage Jayton on Sunday, July 29, in a donkey game, but the following issue is missing, and I have never learned the score.

But I have seen an elephant and heard the hoot owl cry, and I did, there in Jayton, sometime later, see a donkey ball game. Some, I believe, called it jackass ball. I expect there are variations in jackass ball from community to community, depending, I suppose, on the whim of the moment and the availability of jackasses. In the game I saw, the infielders played as usual, but the outfielders were required to ride jackasses, though they could get off to field grounders. Batters went to bat as usual, but if they got a hit, they were required to run the bases mounted. When a batter came to the plate, someone held a jackass for him close by. The jackasses didn't always do what the outfielders and the baserunners needed them to do.

I learn nothing from *The Jayton Chronicle* about playing ball in 1935 and 1936, for I have no issues from those years. I do discover, in the paper for July 29, 1937, that the Jayton team has won a tournament up in Dickens. The April 21, 1938, issue notifies me that Jayton's softball team is playing its first game this very day. The May 5, 1938, paper reports that the businessmen of Jayton are trying to organize an official league, and that must have worked out: the May 19 issue announces the beginning of league play, and I notice that Mr. Coons, the school superintendent, is playing first base. Harmony has entered a team, as have Rising Star and Peacock, and the paper says that "the boys from Golden Pond, Center View, Salt Flats, and Clipper" will also get a team together. On May 26, 1938, it turns out that there are *four* teams from Jayton—the Pirates, the Tigers, the Giants, and the Yankees. By June 9, it appears that there are *two* leagues. One is the Catclaw League, and Jayton has just beaten Girard and McAdoo. Apparently this is the big league competition with towns from other counties. The other league apparently includes only teams from communities within the county. This league has eleven teams—four from Jayton, others from county communities, a team made up of "the negro workers at the oil mill," and another made up of "the Mexicans in the community." According to the June 16, 1938, paper, Clairmont was the early leader in the county league. The June 30 issue tells that Jayton is leading in the Catclaw League, ahead of Girard, Dickens, Spur, Kalgary, and McAdoo.

I was there, I expect, for the home games. A man they called "Sweet Bill" Parnell was the Jayton pitcher. He wore his working cowboy hat.

I don't learn much from 1939. The June 22 paper has a notice of plans to form a four-team league in Jayton. By the time the next week's paper appears, the first games have already been played. Reports on the town league games continue into August. I must have been there for all or most of the games. I cannot imagine missing a game. Those players knew about playing ball before I did, but I can't say exactly what I may have learned from them.

And I cannot account at all for how I might have begun in 1937 to learn about the major leagues, how I might have begun to learn the names of teams, the names of some of the players, who pitched, who hit, who hit well. News did not reach me often or regularly in those days in Jayton.

Specimen box scores from 1937 show me that on Saturday, July 3, Joe DiMaggio hit his 17th home run in the Yankees' 8–3 loss to the Washington Senators, and that on the next day he hit his 18th in a 5–4 win over Washington. On Thursday, July 15, he hit his 23rd home run in a win over the Detroit Tigers. Charley Gehringer, at second base for the Tigers, went one-for-four. On Monday, July 19, DiMaggio hit his 24th home run in a win over Cleveland. On Friday, July 23, though, he was hitless in a game against the St. Louis Browns, while Gehringer went two-for-four in Detroit's 17–4 win over the Boston Red Sox. On Monday, July 28, the Yankees and the Tigers played; the Yankees won, 6–5. DiMaggio went two-for-five, Gehringer three-for-six. Each hit a home run. At the end of the season, Gehringer was the American League batting champion, hitting .371, while DiMaggio was at .346.

But it's unlikely that I would have seen the box scores in 1937. News did not reach me regularly or often in those days. The weekly *Chronicle* carried mostly local sports news. The daily newspaper of choice was the *Fort Worth Star-Telegram*, which already then had a pretty wide circulation around West Texas. (That was still true later. In 1964, I went back to that territory. I had been there a few times on hurried trips since 1939, when my family left, but this trip was an unhurried time to look. I had spent a night in Spur, about 25 miles from Jayton, about five miles from Grandpa's farm, which wasn't his any more. I didn't sleep well and got up by five o'clock to shower and to go for a walk on what I think of as Main Street, though its name is Burlington Avenue, I found the Spur Café open. I went in and sat at one of the stools along the counter. At each place down the counter was a copy of the morning's *Star-Telegram*, neatly

folded. I enjoyed the coffee and the paper and didn't realize until I was almost through that I had apparently displaced all of the regulars by one stool.)

We didn't subscribe to the daily paper then. It would be another three or four years before we saw a newspaper every day. We didn't have a radio until 1938. News didn't reach me regularly or often in those days.

Then how did I know the names of the teams and the names of some of the players? I did know in 1937. I was playing ball in 1937, and sometimes when I played I was Charley Gehringer, and sometimes I was Joe DiMaggio. Sometimes I was just myself. By the time I was in the third grade, I was playing ball as often as I could, and you learn about playing ball. You can always play ball.

In Jayton, it was pretty hard to find eighteen players of similar age and size and ability for a real game. Sometimes, though, you could find ten players, five to a side, and that worked. The team at bat provided a catcher. The team in the field had a pitcher, a first baseman, a shortstop, a leftfielder, and a centerfielder. Any ball hit to right field was an automatic out. With ten or fewer players, you could play "scrub." I never favored that, but it was better than not playing. In "scrub," there are two batters, and everybody else is in the field, and when there was an out, everybody "moved up": the batter who made the out went to right field, the pitcher went to bat, and everyone else moved, too. I didn't care much for "scrub"; it's not a real game, and when you don't have sides, nobody wins.

You could also play ball if there were only two, always sufficient to play catch or to hit and shag flies, though for the latter it was better to have three or four.

And you could play ball if there was only one. For several years, I didn't own a bat, but I did own an old pick handle. Rocks were not scarce in West Texas or in our yard. I was all of the batters on both sides of nine-inning games, hitting rocks into the canyons just beyond our fence. Sometimes, when I really got hold of one for a long hit, I also ran around the house for a home run. Those were real home runs.

Years later, I would still play that game, though I changed positions. When I was in graduate school, we lived in an old apartment building that had thick walls, stuccoed outside. I had a rubber ball about the size of a baseball. Two of our windows were placed so as to leave a reasonable strike zone between them. When I was tired or sleepy, or when work didn't go well, I was both pitchers for a nine-inning game, and I never broke a window.

Later still, I would watch our son at the same work. He drew a strike zone on the garage door and became a pitcher. This was no casual devotion: he pitched at that strike zone for hours and developed remarkable control for a boy. I watched him pitch two no-hitters when he was fifteen. I guess the second, in particular, was the prettiest ball game I ever saw. Not long after that, he decided to give up baseball for golf, which he had also been playing. He and I have never discussed which particular flaws in his character led him to do that.

I don't know how I learned about playing ball, or why, and I don't know how or why I happened upon Charley Gehringer and Joe DiMaggio, how or why I came to pick them out. I'm glad I did. I'm glad I followed their careers. Both are in the Hall of Fame now, and have been for a long while; I gather it wasn't difficult to choose them. Gehringer's lifetime batting average was .320; he knocked in 1427 runs, and his career fielding average was .978. Ty Cobb is supposed to have said of him that "He'd say hello at the start of spring training and goodbye at the end of the season, and the rest of the time he let his bat and glove do all the talking for him." DiMaggio's lifetime batting average was .325; he batted in 1537 runs, and his career

fielding average was .976. In the field, he was always already there where he couldn't have been, making catches where others would have struggled and missed, or never come close.

They were the strong, quiet, graceful knights of my youth. Years later, when Joe married Marilyn Monroe, I thought I knew why, besides just love and lust. Surely it must have seemed that she needed to be rescued. He went on that quest. I guess it didn't work out.

I don't know how I happened to pick them, but I'm glad I did.

Sometimes we can't track back to where all our myths and private imaginings began. Sometimes we don't know the beginning of the story we tell of ourselves, or how and when and where we learned the catechisms we believed in or thought we believed in. Sometimes we don't know how or when or why we learned to be who we wanted to suppose we were being, how we learned to speak as we wanted to suppose we were speaking.

Credentials

I never saw Yankee Stadium or Fenway Park. I never saw Ebbets Field or the Polo Grounds. I never saw the place where the Detroit Tigers played, or the Philadelphia Athletics or the St. Louis Browns or the Chicago White Sox or the Cleveland Indians or the Washington Senators. I never saw the place where the Phillies played or the Cubs or the Reds or the Pirates or the Boston Braves or the Cardinals.

I have never seen a major league game, except on television. In all these years, I have seen, I believe, only two minor league games.

In all these years, I have not seen a complete university or college varsity game.

I have never had extended or systematic or knowledgeable instruction in softball or baseball.

I did see Jayton's softball team play, both in regular games and in a jackass game. As a boy, I played more times than I can remember, or count if I could remember, whether alone or hitting and shagging flies or playing scrub or playing sides. In the army, I played for a season on my company's softball team. From the time my son was eight years old until he was fifteen, I helped to coach boys' baseball teams and so saw more games than I could ever remember. Later, I played in more games than I want to remember on a church team in a slow-pitch softball league.

I have no credentials that a thoughtful, experienced player or a serious fan would approve. When we want or need to think and talk, we seldom get to wait until we have all the right credentials, or until we know all that we might need to know.

Learning the Language

The sneaker in Gregory Djanikian's poem, "How I Learned English," is an immigrant boy "plopped down in the middle" of

> . . . a neighborhood game,

Unnatural and without any moves,
My notions of baseball and America
Growing fuzzier each time I whiffed.

Banished to the outfield because of his inexperience, he
finds himself

    . . . in the path of a ball stung by Joe Barone.
    I watched it closing in
    Clean and untouched, transfixed
    By its easy arc before it hit
    My forehead with a thud.

Unaccustomed to the language, the boy groans, "Oh my shin,
oh my shin." At this, the other players

    . . . dropped from laughter, and there we
                    were
    All of us writhing on the ground for one
                    reason
  Or another.

When the boy laughs, too, he is accepted, and when he is
accepted, he can sneak the language and play the game:

                  . . . the fit
  Of laughter overtook me too,

And that was important, as important
As Joe Barone asking me how I was
Through his tears, picking me up
And dusting me off with hands like swatters,
And though my head felt heavy,
I played on till dusk
Missing flies and pop-ups and grounders
And calling out in desperation things like
"Yours" and "take it," but doing all right,
Tugging at my cap in just the right way,
Crouching low, my feet set,
"Hum baby" sweetly on my lips.

As I began to play ball, I began to learn the language; as I began
to learn the language, I began to learn to play ball.

We've all taken language from baseball, but that's not the
same as the language *of* baseball. In late twentieth-century
America, language from baseball is easy to learn—indeed,
it's unavoidable, and you don't have to be near a ball diamond to use it.

We all know what it means when a working associate says
that "We have to play ball with these people," and we know
when someone is "making a pitch." We know when we've been
"thrown a curve," or maybe worse, a "screwball," and we know
when someone is a screwball. We know, too, when we have
"struck out."

We know what it means when someone asks us to take a

suggestion and "bat it around."

After we've waited "on deck" and it's our time to "step up to the plate," we know that we have to "keep our eye on the ball." Sometimes, we have to "go to bat for" someone, and sometimes we need a "pinch hitter," maybe someone who is a "switch hitter." If my sales program or my advertising campaign doesn't "make the hit" and do so "right off the bat," then my company may bring in a "heavy hitter" to replace me—you know, someone who has a higher "batting average." If that happens, then I've taken my "third strike."

We know, sometimes, how to pull a "squeeze play" on our competitors, and sometimes we know that we've been "caught off base." We know when we should "touch base" with our boss; when we do, we try to "touch all the bases."

We know when to ask for a "raincheck," and we know when we need a "ballpark figure." Sometimes we have to "field questions," some of which "come out of left field."

Some of us like to "play the field." Some of us can't ever "get to first base."

But that's a language from baseball, long since ubiquitous in our conversation. Palmatier and Ray's *Sports Talk, A Dictionary of Sports Metaphors*, lists phrases from baseball that are a part of our common talk. That language is easy enough to learn, though there are some phrases that I wouldn't especially want to hear myself saying. That's not the language of baseball, the language that players speak on the field. I was much slower to learn that language, more hesitant about learning it. Indeed,

I have never learned all of that language, and I have never said some of the words and phrases I did learn. I was startled, disappointed, and hurt when I learned that some ball players sometimes cussed. In the early enchantment, I thought that ball players were always pure. Most things change, and later I did become, if I must say so myself, a pretty fair country cusser in my own right.

I did learn some of this language, and I learned when to use it.

I was pretty quick to learn how and when to say "Hum baby hum baby." That remark, as I understand the language, is something you say only to the pitcher. I should add right away that you have to say this and other statements twice. If you say "Hum baby" only once, it doesn't become a predication, and if you say it three times, that's too many. Also reserved for the pitcher is the advice, "Let him let him hit." Any other player can say this to the pitcher. It is at once advice and encouragement for the pitcher. The statement means something like, "You don't have to do this all by yourself; let the batter hit, and we'll get him out for you."

The expression "Good eye good eye," however, is meant only for batters. Any teammate can say this to the person at bat, and it has implications for both past and future. You say it to congratulate and to reassure the batter when he has just let a bad pitch go by, but the remark is also intended to remind the batter to have a good eye on the next pitch as well.

I learned how and when to say "Let it go let it go." You can say that on more than one occasion. If a batter hits a pop foul or a fly ball that goes foul, and if the first baseman or the third base-man or the rightfielder or the leftfielder or the catcher is dig-ging hard for it, trying to catch it, and if you see that the ball is hopelessly out of reach, you can call out "Let it go let it go." Or if your team is at bat and you're waiting your turn, and if you see almost at the instant the pitcher turns loose of the ball that it's going to be a bad pitch—as you sometimes can since you have a different angle of vision from the batter's—then you can sing out to the batter "Let it go let it go."

I learned how and when to say "Everybody bats everybody bats." You say that after the other side has made the third out and you and your teammates are coming in to bat.

And I learned how and when to say "Way to go way to go." You can say that to the pitcher when he has just "thrown smoke" across the plate. You can say it to a batter when he has just "caught a good piece of it" for a hit. You can say it to any fielder when he has just made a good play, "Way to go way to go."

I never learned all of that language. I never learned to say all that I did learn. I wish I had. Perhaps I would have been a real ball player. Perhaps then I would have known how to say other things, too.

Hidden Beginnings, Uncertain Endings

Each of us is an anthology. We carry around stories, histories, arguments, sermons, proclamations, exclamations, dramas, and creations that we hold. Some of them are complete; some are always being revised. Some of our stories and other literary productions we take to be fixed and final—childhood stories, family lore, early instruction in belief and behavior, whether deliberate or accidental—and we do not easily modify or forsake them, for they are and have been the hitching posts of our lives, whether or not we heard and learned them correctly in the first place, whether or not we have since misremembered them. Others, we revise, perhaps continuously, creating our stories as we go along.

Woven into and around and encrusted upon these personal tales, histories, and other creations are still more, acquired along the way. Jobs and marriage and family and television and current events all bring stories to us that we have to build into our own continuing stories.

Each of us is an anthology of private and public stories and discourses.

And, while there may, of course, be marked similarities among them, we have or acquire our own ways of situating and telling our public and private stories, both those that we think are fixed and those that we revise, and they may be quite different from each other. Each is its own rhetoric; each is told inside its own rhetoric.

That is to say, each story rises out of its own sources, though we may not know all of a story's sources; each takes its own shape and design, though sometimes we borrow available designs; each story is voiced in its own way, though sometimes a manner or style is forced upon us; we situate each story in its own way, though we're not always aware of what leads to a situation; each story has an audience, though sometimes it is only ourselves.

Some stories are too private to tell.

Some stories are too private for us to know—they lie too deep in our souls.

We don't always know what our stories are; those we know, we cannot always account for.

We cannot, for example, always know the origins of our stories. When we go in search of origins, the search often takes us to the place where nothing else can be known.

Oftener than not, we cannot know the ending of our stories, for we are not present as commentators during and after our own deaths. Most stories, however, don't end; their energies persist somehow and somewhere, even if quietly and indirectly. Some stories, I believe, do come to an end.

But most stories don't have a clear beginning and a sure ending.

Still, we can create situations of possibility, sites of convenience, places to start, places to stop.

Getting a ball glove for Christmas, 1937, was not the beginning, but I believe it will serve. I didn't learn until yesterday, though, that the ball-playing story has been ending for some time now.

Scripture

A story doesn't exist without belief. Belief doesn't exist without story. Story and belief are coterminous and isomorphic. I wouldn't know about playing ball and its language unless I was already also believing. Sometimes we come upon or even create for ourselves a story without at the same learning its belief. If the story is momentarily interesting but ultimately not all that significant for us, we can discard it or turn away from it, perhaps without learning its beliefs. If we can't discard or turn away from a story, sometimes we live in it without inquiring about its belief. If we inquire about the belief in which the story grew, sometimes we can't find it, and never know the whole story.

Usually, one begins to learn game, language, and belief so nearly at the same time that it is difficult to differentiate when each came. One way or another, however, foolishly or otherwise, one soon learns language and beliefs if one learns the game, and one soon learns the game if one learns language and belief. Nothing in that is wonderfully surprising. Belief is present early on, however, if not at once, even if it is known only as unarticulated need, even if we are not aware of it, even if we would scoff at such notions. In the beginning, I wouldn't have thought or said belief. In the years since, some exegeses of baseball have been uncommonly appealing to me, without being in my mind either solely sufficient or altogether sufficient. I know that the game is played on green fields with hopes of coming safely home, and I know that vision of a rural Eden is powerful, but the fields I played on were mostly dirt, home kept moving around, and I never found it again in rural West Texas. I know that when you play ball, you can stay young awhile, but my knees gave out, and I learned to age, and after awhile I guessed that I would die. Perhaps we hoped to hold our innocence, but the air and water in West Texas, John Calvin, and my own frailties and failures soon disabused me of that hope. Perhaps we thought we could get outside time on the playing field, and to be sure, you don't have to pay your debts while you're at third base, but the debts don't go away. Perhaps we thought we would find redemption on the playing field, but I found only a pause.

Now, when I go in search of the texts and sources in which I found belief, I can't find all of them. I know that the scripture was cumulative.

When I was in the fourth grade, my family moved to the big city. About a year after that, we started getting a newspaper regularly, and the sports pages became a part of scripture. I studied stories about baseball, and I studied the box scores for all of the games, every day. I continued to do that for years, and knew the players on each team, the batting averages of the players, and the won-lost records of the pitchers. That was essential study.

The discovery of one canonical book preceded our move to the city. I may have found others, but I can recall with certainty only Roy Stokes' *Andy at Yale*. That was my present for Christmas in 1938, and it was the first book I ever owned. I still have it.

Andy at Yale was originally published in 1914 by Sully and Kleintech. The copy that I received in 1938 was published by the World Syndicate Publishing Company of Cleveland. It was the first volume of "The University Series," which never quite became a series. Stokes' plan, apparently, was to follow each of Andy's group of friends to a different Ivy League university. His plan, I judge from the Preface, was not just to tell a story, but also to show that

> Each university has a life peculiarly its own, whether it is at Yale, Harvard, Princeton, or elsewhere. There are certain customs and traditions that are never violated. This forms a large part of the student life. It is what gives each college its individuality.
>
> It has been my endeavor in this series to show something of this life—at least of some aspects of it. I have begun with Yale, not that it is any better known than some of the other institutions, but because of the prominence Yale has always taken in athletics.
>
> And yet this is not a story of college sports, though you will find some attention given to them. I have tried to set down a few incidents in the life of an ordinary student at Yale.
>
> So then you may read how Andy, Chet, Ben and other good fellows, attended at a college preparatory school. How they each chose a different university and how they went there to complete their studies.

> In the present book we take up the life of
> Andy Blair at Yale . . . .

The book takes Andy through his freshman year. A second
book in the projected series, *Chet at Harvard*, was published,
but I haven't read it. The series did not continue, and we
never learn about Ben at Princeton or about Tom at Cornell.
One supposes that the Ivy League universities were clearly the
proper choices as settings for entertainment and for edifica-
tion about university life.

Andy at Yale, at any rate, was clearly my introduction to universities. Football games broadcast on the radio in the fall of
1938 gave me fleeting hints, but *Andy at Yale* was the first manual of instruction for what has been my life. The first lessons
we learn in any arena of interest are powerful lessons, difficult
to forget, difficult to modify. Every university campus I have
known has been in some way disappointing because of *Andy at
Yale*, and I have still never had an office with a fireplace.

Andy's baseball experience in his freshman year at Yale is told
rather briefly, but what's there is enough: when you're nine
years old and reading about your man at Yale playing baseball,
it doesn't get any better. When I look back at the book after all
of these years, I think I see some lessons I learned.

In the fall of 1938, Jayton High School reinstated football
in its program. My brother went out for the team and made
it, playing left guard. Andy Blair goes out for the freshman
football team at Yale after he arrives at school. In the spring,

he goes out for baseball:

> On reaching his apartment, Dunk not having come in, Andy found a notice from the Freshman Athletic Committee, stating that baseball practice would soon start in the indoor cage.
>
> Andy was an enthusiastic player, and had made a good record at Milton. As a freshman he was not eligible for the Yale varsity nine, but he could play on his class team, and he was glad the chance had come to him.

My brother had done it, and *Andy at Yale* had authenticated it: a fellow goes out for a team *after* he comes to school. No word of recruitment or money or athletic scholarship occurs in *Andy at Yale*. A fellow goes out for a team after he comes to school. Even after I learned that it mostly doesn't happen that way, I wanted it to happen that way.

As it turns out, Andy is catcher for the freshman team, and his roommate, Dunk, is the pitcher. Neither they nor their teammates are segregated from the student body. There is no athletes' dormitory, and the athletes are not elsewhere and otherwise, as they have generally been on the campuses I have known. They are known and respected by their classmates. On the evening before their first big game, Andy and Dunk, both edgy about the game, go out for a glass of soda. On the way, they encounter a group of classmates who want the two boys to join them for a night of fun. "Bring them along!" one says. "Down to the rathskeller!" another says. "We'll make a night of it!" says a third. But when the group is reminded of the boys' athletic obligation, they respect their wishes:

> "What's the matter with you fellows, any-how?" demanded another of Andy and Dunk, who were making strenuous efforts to get away. "Don't you love us any more?"
>
> "Sure, better than ever," laughed Andy. "But you know Dunk and I have to pitch and catch in the Princeton freshman game tomorrow, and we—"
>
> "Say no more! I forgot about that," exclaimed the leader. "They can't be burning the midnight incandescents. Let 'em go, fellows. And may we have the honor and pleasure of your company tomorrow night?" he asked, with an elaborate bow.
>
> "If we win—yes," said Dunk.
>
> "It's a bargain, then. Come on, boys, we're late now," and they started off.

And that, I came to think, is the way it's supposed to be.

And what else did I learn? What qualities inhere in a baseball player? I wouldn't have known what or how to say then. Now shall I say "Innocence" and "Pluck"? Yale falls behind early in the game:

> The grandstands were a riot of waving yellow and black, while, on the other side, the blue banners dropped most disconsolately. But it was not for long.
>
> "Come on, boys!" cried the plucky Yale captain. "That's only one run. We only need three out and we'll show 'em what we can do! Every man on the job! Lively! Play ball!"

And that, I came to think, is the way it's supposed to be.

What qualities inhere in a baseball player? Honor, I came to think, and gentlemanliness. On the night before the game, Andy and Dunk are in their room talking, before they set out for the glass of soda I mentioned earlier:

> . . . do you know I'm so nervous over this game that I'm afraid I'll lie awake and toss until morning, and then I won't be much more use than a wet dishrag, as far as my nerve is concerned."
>
> "I feel pretty nearly the same as you do, Andy. Let's sit up a while and talk. I s'pose, though, if we ever make the varsity we'll laugh at the way we're acting now."

"Oh, I don't know," Andy spoke musingly. "Some of these varsity fellows have as bad a case of nerves before a big game as we have now, before our little Freshman one."

"It isn't such a little one!" and Dunk bridled up. "The winning of this game from Princeton means as much to our class, and to Yale, in a way, as though the varsity took a contest. It all counts—for the honor of the old college."

Yale wins the game, and all are gentlemen:

Joyous was the crowd of Yale players as they trooped off the field. The freshmen had opened their season well by defeating Princeton, and the wearers of the orange and black gave their victors a hearty cheer, which was repaid in kind.

And that, I came to think, is the way it's supposed to be.

What else? Nowhere in the account of Andy's baseball experience is there a word of anger or of argument. There is no chewing, no cussing, no spitting, no scratching, no farting. And that, I came to think, is the way it's supposed to be.

But the scripture is cumulative. Later, I would find other beliefs, together with a validation of those I found in *Andy at Yale.*

I learned about universities in 1938. Shortly thereafter, we moved to the big city, and by 1940, I had learned about libraries. Eventually I would learn about the big library downtown, but for a while the branch library within walking distance was more than I could have imagined. Such scriptures I found there, canonical books—I think. Now, I can't be sure. I was reading as fast as I could, and now I can't remember or find all the books that may have taught belief. I remember reading William Heyliger's *Fighting Blood.* The hero was Tarley Nicholas Theodore Ball, otherwise known as TNT Ball, but now I can't find the book. I remember reading Joseph Gollomb's *That Year at Lincoln High.* I remember reading many books by Ralph Henry Barbour. For a while there, he was my favorite, but when I see a list of his books, I can't be sure which ones I read. (And besides, sports stories weren't the only instruction in belief. I learned about brotherly love and courage from Percival Christopher Wren's *Beau Geste,* and from Baroness Orczy's *Scarlet Pimpernel.* I learned that a fellow ought not to call attention to himself, and from all of those western stories I read I learned about fair play and honesty and readiness and all that it takes to be a man according to what I once may have imagined was the Code of the West, which was also about baseball.)

Gollomb's *That Year at Lincoln High* was published by the Macmillan Company in 1918. I must have read it in 1941 or 1942. When I look back at it now, more than fifty years later, little in it seems familiar, only enough to convince me that I did indeed read it. J. Henley Smolett, Jr., dreams of going to

Colborn Prep. His father, realizing that his son has come to be a snob, instead requires him to enter Lincoln High School for his first year. Lincoln is a public school of some 3,000 boys, situated in mid-Manhattan. In this setting, young Smolett enters both an internal and an external struggle.

At first, the hero is, to be sure, snotty and snobbish but he is not impossible. Early on, we learn:

> He felt as though there were two boys within him—a J. Henley he had always known; and another, plain spoken, simple hearted, undistinguished boy whose name would be just a Jim Smolett.

By the end of the book, he has put off the worst of J. Henley and become Jim Smolett.

His external struggle is with Lincoln High; it is personalized in Isadore Smolensky, called Izzy. Their bodies "showed two breeds, worlds apart in history; J. Henley's straight limbed, blond, shapely; Isadore's dark, rather stunted, ungainly and wiry." J. Henley thinks that Izzy dresses like a "Yiddish comedian." Izzy thinks that J. Henley is a "capitalist bloodsucker":

> He was "stuck-up," pampered, and a "goy"— Gentile. Also he was rich. A "goy" was always an oppressor. A rich "goy" was worst of all. He had neither heart nor brains nor human sympathy.

As it turns out, both are bright and both are good athletes. By the end of the book, they are teammates and close friends.

When I look back at the book after all of these years, I think I may, without knowing, have learned a little about politics and about race relations, the latter perhaps especially important since I had lived most of my years in a small town where the few black people lived in almost total isolation from the rest of us, who were mostly Anglo-Saxon and entirely pure and white. I believe I may also have learned a little more about what it takes to be a man.

Early in the book, after his first encounter with Izzy, J. Henley protests his father's decision to send him to public school:

> "Father, you take it for granted that they're all better than I—those east side Jews, the negroes and dagoes," he cried. "You are sure I will learn only good things of them. Well, how about the other way round? Suppose I learn to talk like that specimen tonight? Suppose I catch not their wonderful virtues but their vices? Suppose my mixing with them becomes a mess? It's just possible, you know!"
>
> There was a seriousness in his father's voice which silenced the boy. "That, my

son, is our danger. It is the risk—democ-
racy—life—every one takes. You and I must
take ours!"

But at first, J. Henley knows better. He knows what those others
are like, and knows that it is "typical of that kind to forget their
place. Given the least encouragement these foreigners, these
tenement fellows reached out for the whole world." At first,
he cannot see or know otherwise. His first assembly at his new
school confirms his worst expectations:

> He saw here and there the sons of foreign-
> ers come to America on the tide of immigra-
> tion. Dark faced boys from the east side paro-
> died English with the dialect of vaudeville;
> dark faced boys from mulberry bend mingled
> and mangled English with Italian. There was
> a negro boy from San Juan Hill; nondescript
> Scandinavians; a sprinkling of Syrians, Irish
> and Scotch; several Japanese; a Chinaman.
> "Scum!" muttered J. Henley Smolett, Jr.

But up on the stage, there is that mystery to me if not to J. Henley, "the principal, a well dressed man, in his bearing the mel-
low culture of Harvard and the continental universities. . . ."

At a later assembly, the school's clubs present themselves,
inviting members of the new class into their membership, and

we hear part of their welcoming spiels:

> "—Come in and mix. Come in and develop.
> Come in and learn to work and play with
> your fellow Lincolnites. Everybody welcome.
> Everybody has a shot at being president. The
> best man wins, rich or poor, Jew or Gentile or
> Chinaman, so long as he is a man! Come in
> and become democratic and human whoever
> you are and learn to work and play with your
> fellow man whoever his parents may be or
> whatever may be the cut of his clothes. Come
> in and get the real Lincoln spirit—the spirit
> of America!"

For a while, J. Henley is entangled with the one elitist group that doesn't share these views. Its members look down on all the other students, whose folks "don't know an oyster fork from a corkscrew." The leader of this group remarks that "It takes more than one generation to make an American, and a gentleman."

M. Carton, the teacher who comes to have the greatest significance for J. Henley, expresses a contrary view. At the big track meet, when Katsui, a Japanese student, wins the 100-yard dash for Lincoln High, Mr. Carton says:

> "That's what gives me the deepest joy about

America and its public schools. It's the meeting place of the peoples of the earth and the welding of them. Think of that young Samurai—his father is a former Japanese consul—mingling and hobnobbing with a mixed gathering of young Americans, English, Czechs, Irish, Italians and French—and beating them out as he did! And in the sixty yards an English boy beat him. It's a dream of humanity come true—the federation of the world!"

Lessons and examples of manliness are common. A man doesn't give up. Before trying out publicly for the track team, J. Henley makes a practice run for time around the circuit in Central Park. He is in trouble after the second mile:

J. Henley would have yielded. But it was no longer he who was racing Time but—Jim Smolett. J. Henley had been exorcized a few breaths before. Now it was Jim Smolett who was standing the brunt of that keen agony of muscle, that iron-band pressing in and in on his chest, that sobbing strain for breath.

Then, as he emerged into Central Park West on the home stretch, came "second wind." The knife withdrew from his side; the bands about his chest became elastic, vanished. Great draughts of air flowed into his famished lungs. With it came strength from that mysterious reservoir on which all of us may draw if we only endure long enough.

A man is always fair and straight. After Jim and Izzy have become friends, and after Jim has played basketball against Belton, the leader of the elitist club, who has worn Jim down and beaten him with "crooked work," Izzy shows Jim some moves that aren't quite illegal, but then aren't proper, either:

"Iz, I hope you won't think I'm too goody-good to live. But I do want to be a better sport than that fellow Belton," he said.

"Show me where the book says it's a foul, what I showed you!" Izzy exclaimed indignantly.

"It may not be foul. But it isn't therefore— well, let me call it—fun. Iz, do you ever play chess? My father and I do. I want to win of course. That's part of the fun. But most of it is in the playing. Now, the chess sharps play 'a touch a move'; that is, if you begin making a move, you've got to play it, even if you see you've made a mistake. Dad and I don't mind giving moves back. Why? Because we enjoy the playing so much that each of us wants to win on straight thinking—not on a fluke or a slip-up. Same with basketball. I want to win, yes. But I want to enjoy the game itself. There's no fun in it if you win by any other way but straight basketball. Besides it's a matter of feeling pleasant about it after the game is over, too. I—well, I guess I'm sort of sissy about it!"

Izzy is not a slow student. He sacrifices his own chance to win a long-distance run by hurrying to warn his teammates about the fast-pace decoys the other team is sending out ahead.

A man doesn't call attention to himself, and he doesn't work just for money. Jim designs a superior book cover, and he and Izzy go into business, with Izzy handling most of the production and sales. Jim wants Izzy to have the income, for his father has fallen ill, and Izzy may have to drop out of school, but he is, nevertheless, in a "state of misery," for "the mere business of making money from an invention had seemed an inferior matter," and besides, he doesn't wish to "shout his wares in the public streets."

And a man has pluck. Very young to be a starting pitcher on the high school team, Jim pitches the final championship game. Before the game, Belton, the villainous leader of the elite club, catches Jim and forces him into a fight. Izzy saves him, but Jim's arm is weakened in a wrenching hold. By the last inning, he is exhausted:

> He was standing, swaying, his face a little
> drawn with pain and very white. Mr. Jen-
> nings was whispering in his ear. "Listen, my
> boy. If you don't feel equal I'll take a chance
> on Drake in the box. It's a desperate chance.
> But you're pretty tired, you plucky lad. What
> do you say!" "I—I—wish you'd decide for
> me?" Jim stammered.
>
> Mr. Jennings looked at his haggard face.
> His own face was pale. He signed to a boy
> for a drink of water for Jim. Then as the boy
> took a sip, Mr. Jennings said, his hand on
> Jim's shoulder, "Somewhere in you is the
> needed strength, dear lad! Go—and good
> luck to you! I give you free hand to do any-
> thing you will!"

Jim nodded and walked out on the field. And, of course,
he wins.

I have for a long time supposed, and still do, that after *Andy
at Yale*, Ralph Henry Barbour's books provided my chief written instruction and generated my chief expectations about
school, sports, manliness, and gentlemanliness. Now, after
more than fifty years, though my belief persists, I find it difficult to particularize instructions and expectations. The rea-

son is simple enough: I can't be entirely sure now which of Barbour's books I read all that time ago in that other world.

The checklist of American sports fiction Michael Oriard's *Dreaming of Heroes, American Sports Fiction,* 1868–1980, includes 84 books by Barbour, the earliest published in 1899, the last in 1942. I'm sure that I read a good many of them, but I surely didn't read all. When I have thought of Barbour's books over the years, the books that seem always to come to mind are those in his Yardley Hall series. Harry K. Hudson's *A Bibliography of Hard-Cover Boys' Books* lists eight of his books in that series: *Forward Pass* (1908), *Double Play* (1909), *Winning His Y* (1910), *For Yardley* (1911), *Chance Signals* (1912), *Around the End* (1913), *Guarding His Goal* (1919), and *Fourth Down* (1920). In the same years Barbour published the Yardley Hall series, he also published 22 other books. No matter: I look only at the Yardley Hall books, and I still can't be sure which of them I read.

Double Play seems familiar after these years, but then any of Barbour's books that I read now might seem familiar, even if I didn't read it as a boy, because of similarities among all of the books. *Double Play* introduces early on a hero, whom I think I remember:

> Dan Vinton was fifteen years of age, rather tall, lithe, and long of limb. He had a quickness and certainty of movement—exhibited even in the way in which he stowed his things away—that impressed the observer at

once. Alertness was a prominent characteristic of Dan's; he never shilly-shallied, nor, on the other hand, was he especially impulsive. He had the faculty of making up his mind quickly, and, his decision once reached, he acted promptly and with little loss of effort. Dan's course between two points was always a straight line. All this may have had something to do with the fact that he played an extremely good game of football at the end of the line.

Yardley Hall, I learn or am reminded, is a school of some two hundred and seventy students, situated on a small plateau "about a half-mile from the shore, and commanding a broad view, of Long Island Sound, about half way between Newport and New Haven." I learn, too, or am reminded, that "you will never be able to persuade a Yardley man to acknowledge that any other school approaches it in excellence."

Yardley men, of course, are an excellent breed. In the great snow fight on campus, "It was hand-to-hand out there, and many brave deeds were done and many gallant rescues performed," but the boys are gentlemen, or about to be, and "no one lost his temper, or, if he did, he found it again the next moment." Even at that excellent place, however, and among these excellent men, I gather that some discrimination occurred. Stuart Millener, a classmate,

. . . had never distinguished himself in his studies, but he had worked hard at them and had always managed to remain at peace with the Faculty. He was a fellow who was now and always would be better able to work with his hands than with his brain. And there are plenty of places for that sort in the world. As a first baseman he was a huge success, and there seemed no reason why he should not turn out to be an excellent leader.

Virtues are not hard to find, though; they occur readily among men who, like the physical instructor, are *square*. If the word in later decades came to have other meanings, in the world of Yardley Hall it is a deeply-felt compliment: of a respected faculty member, Dan says that "he was square and just and would treat a fellow white if the fellow showed that he was trying to do his work!"

The climactic moments of the book occur in the last baseball game of the season, between Yardley Hall and its old rival, Broadwood Academy. Dan plays at second base for Yardley Hall. At the beginning of the last inning, Yardley Hall is ahead, 4–3, and the first Broadwood batter strikes out. But then two hits and a walk load the bases. Broadwood's next batter, Kent, is dangerous. He takes two strikes, and then:

Kent got madder still, so mad that he quite
forgot caution and stepped out after the next
ball and, contrary to all law, found it squarely
on the end of his bat. In raced the man on
third, down from second went the next runner, off for second streaked the third, and
away went Kent and the ball simultaneously,
the former for the first bag and the latter, to
all appearances, for somewhere in right cen-
ter-field. Broadwood leaped deliriously and
waved her banners. All this is what the first
moment saw. The next saw a lad poised mid-
way between first base and second and some
yards back of the line, lean high into the air
in the path of the speeding ball, saw the ball
tip the upthrust glove, bound into the air,
and come down in that same glove, saw the
lad race to second and tag that base, and saw
Broadwood's discomfiture and defeat, Yardley's ecstasy and victory!

With an unassisted double play, Dan has saved the day, Yardley
Hall has won, the lads head home, and, Barbour says,

> . . . let us leave them for a time, speeding
> home through the warm, amber glow of
> late afternoon, the wind in their faces and

joy in their hearts, feeling as only boys can
feel after a battle bravely fought and a victory well won.

And that, I thought, is the way it's supposed to be.

But I can't be sure of the text. I'm pretty sure, but not certain, that I read *Double Play* in old times. Barbour wrote 84
books; eight of them were in the Yardley Hall series, and I read
some that weren't in the series. I think Barbour's teachings
were significant to me then and for a long time, but I can't be
sure of the source. How am I to learn how I invented myself,
how the culture invented me, how the culture and I invented
the baseball story, if I can't be sure of the primary texts?

I have not yet mentioned what is clearly the largest and
perhaps the most sacred of the canonical books—that gathering
of however many volumes or pages it takes to hold the records
and statistics that particularize baseball history and baseball
lives. General histories will not tell us, and biographies, if we
had them, cannot be trusted. Hagiographies, which we do have,
will not serve. Not even a good biographical account of life will
be equivalent to performance.

What we do have is the statistics and the records.

Some profess not to understand why followers of baseball are
enthralled by the statistics and records (and the same would be
true of softball students if the records and statistics had been
kept, though we'd never get through them all). To me, the
matter does not seem difficult to comprehend. The records

and statistics particularize the baseball story, and it would not be a story otherwise. We can follow the story season by season or day by day; we can follow teams or individual players. A story exists in its particulars. Absent its particulars, there is no softball story, and the baseball story is the softball story. A story exists in its particulars. We exist in our particulars.

I cannot recapture my first record of the records. It was a little pamphlet or paperback booklet that measured, I'd guess, about three inches by about six inches. I believe the man at the gas station near the square was giving them away, and I believe he gave one to my father, who brought it to me. I'm not sure about that, but I am pretty sure that it was in 1938. I cannot be sure, either, about what all was inside. I think the yearly pennant winners for the major leagues were listed, and the World Series winners, with each season's batting champions and best pitching records. It included lifetime batting averages, at least for those who had hit above .300 for the career, and record-holders for most home runs, singles, doubles, triples, and stolen bases. It included the best lifetime pitching records. I don't know what else was there. I spent considerable time with that little book.

Then, when we had moved to the city and I had gotten used to the library, I discovered that books about baseball there, including those that held the records and statistics, and I thought I had died and gone to heaven. That's when my serious study of baseball began.

That should not be taken to mean that I was constrained

by the facts presented in the records and statistics. I chose my own particulars from all those given. I edited the facts of the baseball story to make my story. I followed the teams and the players whose stories I liked for one reason or another, and made them into my story. I wouldn't claim for a minute that my reasons were always good reasons. I followed the Yankees in the records and in the current box score because Joe DiMaggio was on the team. I followed the Philadelphia Phillies and the St. Louis Browns because they didn't ever seem to win; then, in 1944 and 1950, I was happy when first the Browns, then the Phillies won a pennant, though both of them lost in the Series. I followed Debs Garms, for God's sake, for no particular reason except that he seemed to come out of nowhere to the Pittsburgh Pirates and won the league batting championship with a .355 batting average. I'll not try to account for my choices.

I would not have known to think or to say it then, but when I look back now, I know that as I learned the scripture and the baseball story, I was constructing my story of baseball, which is to say, as well, my scripture.

As I got deeper and deeper into the records and statistics, it eventually came upon me, as I expect it does to most who follow that path, that I needed to determine who the best were, that I needed to figure out who would be on my All-Time All-Star team. That, I think, is a necessary part of story-making, though I didn't know it before. A story is going to have its moments—high points, low points, predictive passages. A story will also have its standards of judgment and value. And so, baseball nuts come sooner or later to name their All-Time All-Star team. I had a lot of trouble with this chore. I kept listing too many players. I couldn't leave some of the names off my list.

Eventually, of course, I decided to compile an All-Time All-Star team for the American League and another for the National League. That helped. I still ended up with too many players, but I couldn't scratch anyone. Occasionally, as the years passed, I added more recent players.

For the American League team, I wanted Mickey Cochrane to be the catcher. I really wanted George Sisler to be on the team, but I had to put Lou Gehrig at first base. At second base, Eddie Collins and Nap Lajoie made strong claims, but for me there was really no choice—it had to be Charley Gehringer. For third, I eventually went modern and picked Brooks Robinson. At shortstop, I would have been pleased enough with Lou Boudreau, and I followed the career of Cecil Travis, who compiled a lifetime batting average of .314 with the Washington Senators, a losing team, but I finally settled on Luke Appling. He was too interesting to leave off. It was reported of him that he could hit foul balls at will, to wear down pitchers, and I believed. You can see the nature of my problem when it comes to picking an outfield. I wanted Joe DiMaggio for center field, but then what would I do with Ty Cobb? I settled the matter by selecting a crew of outfielders without regard to position: Ty Cobb, Joe DiMaggio, Tris Speaker, Babe Ruth, and Joe Jackson, plus the later additions, Carl Yastrzemski and Mickey Mantle. For pitchers, I wanted Walter Johnson, Lefty Grove, Bob Feller,

Whitey Ford, and Red Ruffing, though I privately thought that Walter Johnson could handle the job by himself.

For the National League team, I originally picked Gabby Hartnett for catcher, but later substituted Johnny Bench because my older daughter, who didn't pay much attention to baseball, would come into the room to watch television for a moment whenever Johnny Bench came to bat. At first base, I put Bill Terry, though he would have left off if he had been competing with Gehrig and Sisler. Rogers Hornsby, I thought, had to be the second baseman, and I put Pie Traynor at third. Shortstop was more trouble: the choice had to be Honus Wagner, but I was really distressed to omit Arky Vaughan. For the outfield, I listed Paul Waner first. Someone remarked that he was a graceful baserunner. Someone else is supposed to have replied, "Well, he had to be—he learned to slide gracefully so he wouldn't break the bottle in his pocket." Then I added Joe Medwick and Mel Ott, and later added Stan Musial, Willie Mays, Roberto Clemente, Hank Aaron, and Richie Ashburn. For my patching staff, I chose Carl Hubbell, Christy Matthewson, and Grover Cleveland Alexander, and later added Warren Spahn, Sandy Koufax, and Bob Gibson.

I picked these names from the scriptures. When I had done so, I had named the saints.

If I had known them as they occupied their own lives instead of knowing them as I created them, I might not have included some of them. Well, Christy Matthewson and Walter Johnson would qualify, and Joe DiMaggio and Charley Geh-

ringer. But some or many of the others wouldn't have fit into
Roy Stokes' book, or Gollomb's, or any of Ralph Henry Barbour's books. Some of them were louts. Some were drunks.
Some, no doubt, were coarse, and some were mean. Against
the scripture I wanted to believe had accumulated and the
behavior it required, every locker room I was ever in was a
violation, and most playing fields were disappointments. Even
if they were loutish, drunk, coarse, and mean to begin with,
they played good baseball, and I thought that was enough. I
thought that baseball might even cleanse and purify them. I
imagined them all, even Ty Cobb, to fit the scripture I had
found and believed. Perhaps, after all, since I was in the beginning a little timid and often fearful, and am still, I was only
looking for a shining place where I would be free and safe.

Liturgy

I continued to believe for a long time. Perhaps I still do. Perhaps my faith wasn't strong enough. At least, it didn't match
pretty Jo Anne's faith, though I never learned for sure whether
she had all the faith necessary at the outset or married extra
faith later.

She had an open, pretty face and a bright and beautiful
smile, and she was, I thought, organized in an altogether lovely
sort of way, but she was Baptist. We dated a few times in the
summer after we graduated high school, but her faith over-
came me. She and her family didn't believe in going to movies,
or in smoking, or in dancing, or in drinking. I couldn't think

of anything for us to do on dates except go to church or play miniature golf, but church isn't always available, and you can only play miniature golf so many times. After a little while, we parted. Later, I heard that she had married an ardent softball player—at home plate, attended by uniformed teammates. She and her groom, someone told me, came to the altar—that is, home plate—under crossed bats held aloft by the teammates. I could never have matched that.

I did learn to genuflect along the way. When I played second base for a while, opposite a really good shortstop, I learned that when a runner was on first base and the batter hit a ground ball toward me, I would need to bow, to take the ball surely in hand, and to genuflect to the shortstop, because he was by that time going to be coming full speed toward second base and would expect my toss to arrive at the sacramental moment as he stepped on the bag, ready to throw to first base for the double play.

I continued to believe for a long time. Perhaps I still do. My belief, I guess, was never as strong, my faith never as wide or as deep, as all that others achieved. In the introduction to his book, *Baseball and the Pursuit of Innocence*, Richard Skolnik encapsulates most of the myths and hopes that we have found in baseball:

> In the following chapters the case is presented for baseball's role as a symbol for an America not but dimly recalled. It is in this

connection that the related notions of pasto-
ralism, simplicity, and innocence, so closely
interwoven into the sport, are identified and
analyzed. The fields of green, the summer
sun, the rural cadences, the initiation into
the game of young sons and daughters by
fathers all resonate with those themes. Not
content to invoke the past, baseball lavishes
attention upon it and is ever respectful of its
early days. Memories remain exceptionally
vivid, statistical comparisons abound while
the dialogue between present and past stays
consistently rich, fresh, and rewarding.

Baseball's uncommon regard for order
and regularity recalls a past in which formal
structures reflected a world more rigid, more
sharply defined. Baseball's demanding moral
order appears suited to a traditional age, one
that defined and enforced appropriate behavior, prescribed obligations, and fixed individual responsibilities. Finally, baseball's grip on
the popular imagination was enhanced, made
more credible because the game in many
ways appeared familiar, its players, strategies,
and rhythms recognized extensions of the
fabric and flow of daily, commonplace events.
Thus baseball invites us to suspend our sense

of time, delight in our youth, partake in an
orderly universe, relish the natural freshness
and hope of spring, and take comfort in the
workings of the familiar.

Maybe. Yes, I guess so. At any rate, I continued to believe for a
long still. Perhaps I still do. For a long time, I continued, more
or less faithfully, to perform the acts that the scripture seemed
to demand of me. You are supposed to bow and genuflect to
the shortstop if you want to turn the double play.

When you are fielding a ground ball, you keep the ball in
front of you.

You back up whomever you are supposed to back up.

Outfielders coming in and infielders going back for a short
high fly are supposed to let each other know who will make
the catch.

When you're the middle man in a double play, you're supposed to touch second base while the ball is in your hand, not
just come close.

If you are a baserunner coming from first base on a potential
double play, you are supposed to discourage the infielder at
second base from making a throw to first base.

You're supposed to know how many outs there are.

If you're in the outfield, you're supposed to hit the cutoff
man on throws back to the infield.

You're not supposed to take too wide a turn at first base after
running out a hit.

If you're a runner on base and batter hits a deep fly, you're supposed to go back to the base and tag up rather than moving halfway to the next base.

If you're a runner coming from third base to home and the ball arrives by the time you do, you're supposed to discourage the catcher from holding on to it.

You are supposed to be composed and ready for whatever comes.

A team is supposed to have eight regular players who know their territory, play it every day, and get better each day until age wins. Joe DiMaggio and Charley Gehringer didn't take turns with anyone.

If you are going to bunt, you're supposed to know how and you're supposed to know where to put it.

You are supposed to refrain from quarreling, cussing, spitting, and scratching.

You are supposed to behave like a gentleman.

You don't show off if you hit a home run.

You are not supposed to go down with the bat on your shoulder.

I guess I've forgotten or never knew all the other acts that the scripture requires of us. There's a lot to learn, whether, as Conrad Hilberry's poem, "Instruction," tells us, by instruction or by oneself:

> The coach has taught her how to swing,
> run bases, slide, how to throw

to second, flip off her mask for fouls.

Now, on her own, she studies
how to knock the dirt out of her cleats,
hitch up her pants, miss her shoulder
with a stream of spit, bump
her fist into her catcher's mitt,
and stare incredulously at the ump.

And William Matthews, in his poem, "The Hummer," tells
about the practice we need:

> First he drew a strike zone
> on the toolshed door, and then
> he battered against it all summer
> a balding tennis ball, wetted
> in a puddle he tended under
> an outdoor faucet: that way
> he could see, at first, exactly
> where each pitch struck.
> Late in the game the door
> was solidly blotched and
> calling the corners was fierce
> enough moral work for any
> man he might grow up to be.
> His stark rules made it hard
> to win, and made him finish

any game he started, no matter
if he'd lost it early.
Some days he pitched
six games, the last in dusk,
in tears, in rage, in the blue
blackening joy of obsession.
If he could have been also
the batter, he would have been
trying to stay alive . . . .

You're supposed to practice, Richard Jackson says in "Center Field," because

. . . we have only the uncertain hang time
of a fly ball to decide how to position
                                        ourselves,
to find the right words for our love,
to turn towards home as the night falls, as
                                        the ball,
as the loves, the deaths we grab for our own.

Playing Ball

While I was playing ball, others were thinking momentous thoughts, and I was only playing ball. I thought I had learned or was learning the language, but that wasn't so. I never learned all of the language, but I never escaped the language, even the parts I didn't know. Michael Oriard's study, *Sporting With the*

Gods: the Rhetoric of Play and Game in American Culture, takes the language further than I would have guessed when I was playing ball, to a study of the "specific rhetoric of sport, play, and game, and my sense of that rhetoric's most significant functions." Oriard traces the "histories of a number of rhetorical figures—images, similes, metaphors, analogies—that express heroic codes, strategies of survival, states of being, life itself as 'sport,' 'game,' or 'play.'" He follows a "handful of specific tropes" (how long before I would know what that word might mean?) through cultural history to learn their significance:

> The popular rhetoric of "play" and "games,"
> in other words, is profoundly ideological, yet
> its relationship to political power is not at all
> straightforward. The function of rhetoric is to
> persuade. The rhetorical figures I discuss are
> sometimes popular fantasies of an idealized
> past or future, sometimes more ambivalent
> wrestling with an intransigent present; they
> express values, hopes, fears, desires, anxieties,
> even entire social philosophies or world views.
> Ultimately, the linguistic construction of life
> as game or play has served to reinforce exist-
> ing power relations, but that generalization
> does not adequately account for the messier
> relations of language and power. Sometimes
> the sporting rhetoric overtly resists the pre-

vailing political power of the day; sometimes
it endorses, promotes, and enhances it;
sometimes it seems to resist but tacitly aug-
ments the power arrangements through its
evasion. And sometimes, though not all that
often, it is evoked by those in power in ways
meant to consolidate that power. The result-
ing ambiguity and confusion reveal a culture
often at odds with itself.

I dispute nothing of this now, and I knew nothing of this then,
when, at age fifteen, I played third base for a team made up of
newspaper carriers in a city softball league. That summer of
1945 was a sweet time: the trees cast a blue shade along Cleckler
Street, the war was just about over, my brother was safe, I was
deeply in love several times, and I was playing ball regularly.

I had gotten a new glove earlier in the year. The old one was
just about used up. The new glove delighted me, but it was not
as momentous as the first. Of much the same design as my old
glove, it was bigger and better padded. The thick thumb, the
thick heel, and the thick little finger made a nice pocket for
the ball, but the fingers were still not attached to each other,
except for the thumb and index finger.

Pretty soon, Joe DiMaggio came back from the war, and our
careers once again went on together, his a little faster and a
little more noticeably. Mine had its little moments. I remember a splendid double play when a hard line drive came to me

at third so fast that I was able to double up a runner who had taken too much lead at first. What a time that was. I remember a splendid home run I hit, perhaps the best, most relaxed long hit I would ever get. The trees behind the backstop made blue shade, and the field was golden in the light of a perfect late spring day. What a time that was. I'm sorry to report that I do not have records of my batting average and fielding average.

By the fall of 1946, it became necessary for me to take some time off from my ball-playing career, as it had for Joe. By that time, I was in college and working as many hours a week as I could manage. I didn't have much time. I had lost my softball connections. I wasn't good enough for a college team, though of course I would have been if they had just noticed.

I did not handle the mixture of college, work, and poverty very well, and so my academic career slowed down almost as much as my ball-playing career. After the end of my junior year, I took the fall semester of 1950 off from school to try to make some more money. As it turned out, that was not a good semester to be out of school. I was drafted, went through basic training, and went to Germany with the 57th Medium Tank Battalion, part of the 2nd Armored Division.

That afforded me the chance for a brief comeback. The Headquarters and Service Company had a softball team, and I played third base. Company A, down the street, also had a team. That team would go on to win the European Theater softball championship. We played them three times. None of us ever got a hit. They could have beat us with just the pitcher and the catcher. When I batted against that Company A pitcher, I never did get a chance to swing and miss—the ball was already in the catcher's mitt before I could get the bat around. Once I tried to throw my body in front of the pitch, but I was late with that, too. I didn't get a new glove.

Then came a long hiatus in my ball-playing career. Indeed, I decided that it was over. When I came back from the army, I finished school, and then went on through graduate school without, I think, ever seeing a real softball or baseball. But I do remember October 8, 1956, and the fifth game of the World Series between the Dodgers and the Yankees. Sal Maglie pitched a five-hitter for Brooklyn, but Don Larsen pitched a perfect game. I had come home from school for lunch and we watched the game, and I got more fidgety as the game went on and Larsen hadn't given up any hits or walks. I was in a graduate class that met at one o'clock and I couldn't afford to miss it, but Larsen wasn't giving up any hits or walks. By the 7th inning, it was time for me to go back for class, but Larsen wasn't giving up any hits or walks. Finally, I said, "The hell with it," and watched the game. Then I raced back to school, where I met the professor: he'd stayed at home to watch, too.

For a long time, though, I only played ball second-hand, watching games on television and, for seven or eight years, coaching or helping to coach a boys, baseball team.

But I would make a comeback.

Rounding First and Heading Home

An editorial in the April 4, 1995, issue of the local newspaper announced that "The strike is over. The season is delayed. The real players are coming April 26. And yet nothing has been accomplished." The strike lasted 234 days, and at the end there was still no lasting work agreement. Those involved achieved nothing "except to raise the level of acrimony between the players and the owners and to further sunder the big-league game from the affections of its fans." Then the editorial continued:

> The temptation at this point is to tell them when they come asking us to watch: "Sorry, boys. We're just too busy."
> That is not how it was supposed to be.
> Baseball has long offered us a playing field of perfect unreality.
>
> While life might be confusing, unjust, and out of control, the game itself has stayed as trim as its diamond, with defeats clearly defined and victories equally so. It has provided a kind of parallel dimension that seems real and important when we need it to be but is actually comfortably inconsequential . . . .

For a little while, that made sense to me, and the argument that the editorial presents may be a lasting argument. In the winter of 1994–1995 and in the spring of 1995, on the infrequent occasions when I thought about baseball and the strike, I was generally astonished and outraged by the behavior of both parties. Sometimes, I would put down the newspaper and tell myself that I just didn't much care any more.

And I guess I don't, but it's not because of the strike.

When I stopped to think and to look back, I realized that I had started letting go of baseball, or of the baseball story, or of the story I had made of baseball a long time ago.

How long ago was it, I wondered, that I quit reading the sports pages and studying the box scores? One day I was browsing in *The Baseball Encyclopedia*, enjoying once again seeing the names and figures from old time, when I realized that I was coming upon a lot of "modern" names that meant little or nothing to me. A little checking back and forth showed me that I must have quit paying attention to rosters, records, and daily box scores somewhere along in the early 1960s. That's one pretty sure sign that I wasn't as close to the baseball story as I had thought, and hadn't been for a long time.

I realized then, too, that I had long since quit watching games on television, probably as far back as fifteen years ago.

I had, I began to realize, been letting go of the baseball story for a long time.

But I still made a comeback that lasted for three or four years. When the church I was attending at the time organized a softball team and joined a city slow-pitch league, I was ready. When the team was together and ready to play, we still needed prayer and more speed in the outfield, and I was playing second base, though a little later I shifted over to first base, fully expecting all ground balls to bounce eyeward, groinward, goneward, but not gloveward. I had thought, when I joined the team, that if I did some wind sprints and sweated a lot, I would soon round into shape. Didn't happen, but I was playing ball again, and I loved it.

In 1995, looking back, I realize that something else had been happening for a long time: I had rounded first and was heading home, wanting only to get safely home.

I can tell about slow-pitch softball pretty quickly. When I batted against that Company A pitcher, sometimes the catcher had already thrown the ball back to him before I got my bat around. In slow-pitch softball, I could go to bat, take my place in the batter's box and watch the pitcher let go of the ball, and then I could put my bat down, spit some, scratch a while, check where the fielders were, and still have time to pick up my bat and to get a hit when the ball reached me.

I didn't get a new glove, but slow-pitch softball pretty well kept me off the streets until I was forty-five. By that time, I had noticed that if I were going to make it as far as second base, I was going to have to hit the ball far enough for a home run. I had noticed that my teammates were inquiring about my health pretty regularly, before every game at first, then in between innings as the season progressed.

And in 1996, looking back, I realized that I had rounded first and was heading home, wanting only to get safely home. And that's not the direction you're supposed to go.

When I was young and could imagine that my feet were nimble, my hands were quick, and my eyes were sharp, I played third base. By the time I signed up for slow-pitch softball, I realized that while of course I was still nimble, quick, and sharp, I was perhaps not quite as nimble, quick, and sharp as I had been, and so I moved over to second base. As they say in baseball language, I had lost a step or two. My son was, for God's sake, at third. After the first year of slow-pitch softball, I moved to first base. I had lost another step or two, and even Mickey Mantle and Stan Musial and Carl Yastrzemski had moved from their positions to first base in the last years.

I was, you see, rounding first and heading home, needing to reach the safety of home.

After that, I didn't play any more. Nothing is left of my playing career, unless it's the harm I may have done to my knees. I own few artifacts. I have my old glove that I got for Christmas in 1937. I have my son's first glove. It needs to be cleaned and oiled. I did have a baseball signed by Hank Aaron, but I gave it to my son. I have a few bats left over from the boys' teams I coached. I have the beat-up glove that I used in slow-pitch softball.

It wasn't the strike. I had been letting go for a long time. The story is almost over.

Stories End, But They Don't Go Away

I call them back, but they don't come. I call them back, the great ones, the interesting ones—Dizzy Dean, Johnny Vander Meer, Ed Delahanty, Cool Papa Bell, Willie Keeler, Lefty Gomez, Satchel Paige, George Case, Pee Wee Reese, Jackie Robinson, Rube Marquard, Josh Gibson, Lloyd Waner, Three Finger Brown, Chief Bender, Van Lingle Mungo—but they don't come. If they did, I wouldn't like some of them. I have often played in the wrong league, on the wrong diamond, with the wrong players.

I made the story of baseball my way, not often consonant with other wishes, perceptions, and realities. I do not regret that. In my story, those high moments of release and joy when you first run onto the playing field are about as close to exaltation as some of us ever get, and some innings were dear and sweet.

I was an uncommonly long while learning that I didn't fit in a Ralph Henry Barbour book, not so long learning that I didn't fit in the major-league baseball story, either: my eyes were not sure enough, my arm was not strong enough, and my spirit, if that's what it was, was not intense enough or aggressive enough.

I didn't know any of that at first, and I had already commenced making my story of baseball.

When you begin to construct your story, in whatever territory with whatever materials, you're already inside a story that tells you which story to construct. I cannot call back, find, retrace, or uncover the story or stories that took me to my story of playing ball. I daresay that there was nothing all that complex;

mostly it was what happened if you were a male growing up in a particular time and a particular place. And it wasn't all my doing: baseball had its own compelling attractions, not least of which was that sense of release into a self-controlled arena that was small enough to handle, unlike that world out there off the ball diamond, where people die.

One way or another, we make the story or stories that will have the shape and manner and extent that we want, or can at least tolerate. I was already enchanted by the time I was enchanted, and I began to author the story with myself in it. All the players would be pure and true and good. All the fields would be sweet and untroubled. We would all be as gallant as Joe DiMaggio and Christy Matthewson and Beau Geste.

I discovered, looking back, that I had begun letting go of the story earlier than I had thought. Perhaps that's only because I kept getting older, but I don't much believe that merely aging accounts for our revisions of our stories or for our willingness, sometimes, to change stories, as I expect we do in any successful educational enterprise. Revision and change can occur without much aging, and aging can occur without much or any revision and change.

Some of us are not able or willing to revise and to change stories, because we don't know that we exist in stories. Some of us believe that we're already in the truth, not in stories, and so there is no need or occasion to change.

My story of baseball was trivial enough, but I can't claim that I have traded it in for a better. Many stories of baseball exist around us and in use, more than I could ever count, let alone the stories out there that tell how the world was, is, and will be.

We exist in stories, as stories, stories that we tell ourselves, stories that we tell others. Sometimes we don't know that we've made a story and are inside it. Sometimes we don't know that our story is like other people's stories. Sometimes we don't know that our story is quite different from other people's stories. Sometimes we are self-deceived and strangers to the truth. Sometimes we don't know that a story has ended: we cling to our story, even seek to force it upon others, as some now still want to make the world and all of us in it look like a Norman Rockwell *Saturday Evening Post* cover.

But even if they end, stories don't go away. The libraries of stories and the debris of still more are all around us all of the time. Others would have made out the line-up for a different set of All-Time All-Star teams. I would have made out a different line-up myself at another time so as to save room for Arky Vaughan. Others wouldn't have noticed All-Time All-Star teams at all.

I can, I guess, get along without the baseball story now. I didn't have it right at the outset, even if it was sweet. But how do you surrender a story so central to your life that you can't even ask whether it's right or wrong? The first, or early, lessons that we learn are powerful. We usually don't know where any story begins, and usually there is no single moment when it ends, even if we know that it ends. Often, we go on speaking in a story after it ends. The story is the world we live in, and we are always in a story that we take as truth.

Exactly how did I learn my catechism? I don't know. Why was sport part of it? I don't know.

When a fellow learns that his catechism is wrong, does that mean that he's through with it? Of course not. Not necessarily. Life without your catechism, without your first lessons, is hard. It's hard, even if you don't know it, to acquire a story, and worse, even if you don't know it, to surrender a story. Perhaps you don't.

Stories end. Time comes when we no longer give them our primary focus or chief attention, though they may still direct us quietly, especially when we're not paying attention. My story of baseball is a volume that I try to put away in a corner of my mind. If I want fair play and gentlemanliness and devotion, I'll have to make them myself and not assume that they are already present in my story, a little mistaken volume, even if it somehow still seems to be a story to another.

Stories end. They no longer direct us, except quietly. I will not be able to play on a team alongside Joe DiMaggio or Charley Gehringer or Christy Matthewson or Walter Johnson. But stories, even if we give them up, remain as memory and energy. Stories persist. My story of baseball rubs against and erodes the dollar baseball story that owners and players create, and their dollar baseball story rubs against and erodes my story. Stories, I nevertheless think, should be known and saved.

How do I know the story is over? It's no longer generative

for me, if it ever was. The story, at best, could only be replicative, and that's not altogether possible. The story rests upon and creates sadness and untruth. I cannot ever be the second baseman playing on Joe DiMaggio's team. Stories come to an end. They may be inert, but they seldom if ever lose all of their energy. Ralph Henry Barbour's story of baseball was not only already over when he wrote it: it never was, but it was generative for me. Dead stories, silent stories, illusory stories, wrong stories do come to life. Whether that is good or bad, right or wrong, depends, I guess, upon whether or not we are watching, paying attention, learning stories.

I let my story of baseball go, watched it wind down, let it peter out, not because I was disgusted by the dollar story of the strike, but because the story was over for me. My story was complete: it had begun somewhere, it existed a while, and it was over. The time of my story is over. New time waits for those who can go there. The self that made that story is gone.

I would not, if I could, write an elegy for time past or for the story that was. Such small heroes we had. Such small heroes we were, and all we had. I'm the only one I had to send onto the field to play in my place.

I Never Played Catch With My Daughter

Yesterday, Kate told me she had outed someone in her ball game on Saturday.

She didn't linger long after telling me. She was pretty busy doing things. After she left the room, her mother explained that Kate had made a good play at second base, putting a runner out. Her mother also said that Kate had gotten a good hit, really walloping one.

Kate is five years old, about to be six. Her mother is my younger daughter. I came to understand that Kate is playing now on a girls' stickball team. In stickball, the pitcher doesn't pitch the ball to the batter. The ball is placed on top of a little post, and the batter swings away. I gather that stickball moves along pretty fast. A five-year old pitcher isn't likely to get the ball over the plate or near the batter. All those bad pitches slow the game down a lot, and, I'm told, pitching puts a lot of pressure on youngsters.

I want to argue, but I can't argue with my daughter. She won't let me smoke in her house, and I don't argue about that. I want to argue this time, though. I want to say that pressure is part of the game, that you're supposed to take responsibility for whatever fix you get yourself into, that if you're pitching and you fall behind the batter, three balls, no strikes, then you've got to keep pitching.

I want to argue, but I can't. Every youngster will have moments, days, years of pressure anyway. We don't need to add more pressure needlessly. Pressure for the sake of a silly game is needless pressure.

I want to argue that hitting a ball that's sitting still on top of a little stick isn't playing ball. I can't argue with her. I argue with myself. "Who says so?" I ask myself. "Who appointed you God?" I ask myself. I know that if it's a good game and the kids play hard and enjoy playing, then it's all right, but I mutter to myself, "It still isn't the same as playing ball."

I can't argue because, after all, I know that it doesn't have to be the same as playing ball the way I wanted playing ball to be, though it seldom was.

I may have learned some of the lessons of my boyhood well. I may even have learned some of the lessons about playing ball well. I may have created laws and rules and expectations out of what was only the trash and trivia and clutter of the culture that I had stored in my mind. I may even have done a good job of creating my story of baseball.

But it wasn't much of a story, and once I had created it, I kept telling it wrong and doing it wrong.

I don't believe that I exaggerate when I say that as my son was growing up, we spent hours playing one kind of ball or another. For a year or so, in season, after I put up a hoop on the garage, we flirted with basketball. That was fun, but not our game. From the time he was in junior high school until his last year of college, we devoted some portion of each fall to throwing a football, each of us, in our time, making miraculous catches. We gave considerable time to tossing a frisbee, both short and long distance. But before, during, and after all of that, we played catch. When you are playing catch, you are throwing either a baseball or a softball, and it didn't matter to us which. We took turns being the pitcher. We threw high fly balls to each other. We threw grounders to each other. We played catch. From the time he was three years old until he finished college, we played catch.

But I didn't play catch with my two daughters.

I didn't decide not to play catch with my daughters. I didn't inquire whether or not I might play catch with my daughters. I just didn't play catch with my daughters. I guess I had already taught myself to know that this was the way things are supposed to be. I guess I had already learned the scripture and the liturgy. I guess I had long since learned from Ralph Henry Barbour and Zane Grey and P.C. Wren how to create and to be a code of the West and a story of baseball, how to create a code of beliefs, a catechism, a liturgy of practices, and of expectations about how things are supposed to be.

Now, all these years later, I think of the time with them that I lost. I do not regret the time I spent playing catch with my son. I would not surrender a minute. But I wonder about the time I lost with them. Now, all these years later, when I think of the way things are supposed to be, I wonder, "Who says so?"

What monstrous knowledge, what sweet knowledge misunderstood and misused, what ignorance, what thoughtlessness did I use to make my story of baseball, myself? I made codes and practices and expectations out of little shards of experience, and imagined that they were the truth of how things were supposed to be. Now, all these years later, I ask, "Who appointed you to be the Almighty?" I didn't play catch with my daughters.

The story I made of baseball has nothing much to start with, and when I had made it, I kept telling it wrong and doing it wrong. What else? What else?

Still, in the back of my car, I keep a softball and a beat-up glove, in case there's need. I guess it's unlikely that we'll all play catch together, but I keep the glove and ball close by in case someone should want to play catch, in case some umpire somewhere should cry, "Play ball!" We could play until dark.

The Rock-Kicking Championship
of the Whole World,
Now and Forevermore

Unlike baseball, for the most splendid example, rock-kicking is not well documented in its history, in its great moments, or in the particulars of great careers or individual achievements. Both its great champions and their great feats are lost to our memory. The great single kicks are mostly gone from our minds. Kicking averages, for distance, accuracy, and beauty, were, so far as I am able to tell, never kept. The popularity of the sport is, though limited for reasons I will suggest later, probably much wider than we know. Its significance for us, too, is probably not yet fully recognized. Given our common proclivity for plowing up the past and covering it over with concrete, the sport may, indeed, be obsolescent for lack of rocks. We have, then, I think, all the more reason to take a moment's notice now of the sport's history, its rules of conduct, its equipment, its playing arenas, the needs that occasion the sport, and the satisfactions that derive from it.

But all present should know that, while I do wish to claim a modest expertise, I am not a specialist in the history, conditions, or philosophical nature of the sport. Neither am I, for all my sometime zeal in rock-kicking, antagonistic or indifferent to other sports.

As I was growing up, I was an ardent, though inadequately motivated, jock, clear through to my bone marrow. Nothing came of it, but I need to tell a little about my career as a near-athlete so you will know at the outset that my interest in rock-kicking did not come at the expense of love for other sports.

When I first went to school, my family lived in a town that claimed some 700 souls in population—that doesn't include Boone Bilberry, who, according to the Baptists, didn't have a soul. I went to a school in that little town through the fifth grade. My brother was five years older than I. When he was in the ninth grade, Jayton High School decided that it would field a football team for the first time in history. If you are demographically agile, you'll soon reckon that a town of 700 souls—not counting Boone Bilberry—wouldn't have a large number of high school age males. At any rate, my brother played on the varsity team while he was in the ninth grade and again in the tenth grade until we moved to the city.

Though baseball was my first love, football was what a young male did in a small West Texas town. I expected to be a football player. I had some natural though untutored ability, and probably would have been a football player in that small town. But we moved to the city, and there were more folks, and some of them were a whole lot larger. By the time I was a junior in high school, I had my full height, six feet, but I only weighed 135 pounds and somewhere had acquired an entirely unjustified regard for the well-being of my ungainly person, and so I abandoned football. Thereafter, I was mostly a runner, though I played baseball and softball. Later I played on an Army softball team, and still later I played on a church softball team until the behavior of my knees, the instruction of my doctor, and the suggestions of my teammates caused me to retire at 45. I still regret deeply that I didn't turn out to be Joe DiMaggio.

But through it all there was rock-kicking, and if there were annals as complete as there are for baseball, I think I would have a sure, though modest, place in the records. I have practiced faithfully since I was first able to kick, and I still practice every day. I have played the game faithfully. I have made scattershot kicks, and I have made thrilling kicks. I have lost, and I have been in contention all the way.

As I said upon commencing, the history of the game is not well documented. But while the literature is sparse, we can assume from what survives that rock-kicking is at least coterminous with the development of welltoed shoes, though the literature shows that some were devout rockkickers while sandals and some forms of moccasins were still common. The literature that does survive includes both arcane work not hitherto accessible and texts not previously interpreted correctly. The fourteenth chapter of Job (verse 18) tells of an early rock-kicker:

> And surely the mountain falling cometh
> to nought, and the rock is removed out
> of his place.

Earlier than that, however, I Kings 19:11 tells of the origins of rocks for the kicker:

> . . . and behold the Lord passed by, and a
> great and strong wind rent the mountains,
> and brake in pieces the rock before the
> Lord . . . .

And Deuteronomy 32:31 tells of early discriminations among rocks by kickers:

> . . . their Rock is not as our Rock . . . .

Near our own time, of course, Bob Dylan's "Like a Rolling Stone" is a celebration of the game, though it clearly speaks for the unpracticed and unartful:

> How does it feel
> to be on your own

with no direction home
like a complete unknown
like a rolling stone.

No thoughtful practitioner of the sport would be entirely unaware of direction; still one is grateful for such praise as one can find for the rolling stone. Psalm 91:11-12 clearly reveals the perils of rock-kicking and the watchfulness of the Lord in the days before the welltoed shoe:

> For he shall give angels charge over thee, to keep thee in all thy ways. They shall bear thee up in their hands, lest thou dash thy foot against a stone.

A little earlier I mentioned literature not previously accessible. I mean to refer, for example, to stone fragments found near Athens, the message carved upon them reinforced by later fragments found just up from the coast in Turkey, both telling the rest of the story of Sisyphus. Long lost to us was the account they give of the other reason for his ordeal: he was condemned to eternal frustration with the rock when it was found that he had intended to take it to the top of the mountain in order to improve his lie.

That brings me to an account of the rules and equipment of the contemporary sport. Except for two items, I want to defer discussion of the rules until just a little later. I have already alluded to the first and most significant rule in my reference to the complete Sisyphus story: in rock-kicking, before all else, one does not improve one's lie. The rock must be kicked where it is. The second regulatory item I'll mention now is not a rule, but a differentiation among rules. There are, in fact, two games. My chief concern now is with the isolated rock-kick, or with distinctly different kicks of distinctly different rocks for distance, accuracy, and beauty. The other game is serial rock-kicking, in which one selects a single rock and kicks it to one's actual destination, as for example, kicking a rock home from the campus. I'll not discuss this second game here except to say that in it, too, the cardinal rule is not to improve one's lie. I'll return to the rules a little later.

Equipment, I'm glad to say, is simple. One needs only *two shoes* and rocks. Two shoes are essential: those truly devoted to the sport will want to be skilled with both feet. It is, at any rate, a virtual necessity. Since one cannot improve one's lie, and since rocks will come to rest in strange places, it is important to be able to get at them with either foot. The kind of shoes one wears is ultimately irrelevant—devoted practice and performance can produce a good kick with any kind of shoe, though some, of course, give greater assurance than others. You can, if you give the move the intensity of vision and kinetic concentration it deserves, get a good kick, for example, with dress shoes, and the slick soles and pointy toes add a certain risk and challenge to the event. For longterm, sustained kicking, though, other shoes are better. In general, you want a rounded toe with a thick sole—the best kicks, I think, come off the sole of the shoe, not the toe above the sole. Devotion and practice are the keys to good kicking, however, and the good kicker will get good kicks with bad shoes, just as he or she will sometimes get a bad kick off a good shoe. I've found three kinds of footwear most efficient. I suppose I'm still fondest of the first, which I wore when I was first learning the game. I'm referring to old-fashioned tennis shoes—we called them tenny shoes—with thick soles, the kind that laced up around the ankles. The thick soles gave a tough, rounded, resilient surface for striking the rock, and besides, when my mother finally said I could put on my new tenny shoes in the spring, they made me feel light and fast, and I thought I could kick any rock anywhere. I'm reluctant to admit it, but the second form of footwear I've found particularly good is army combat boots. They gave good support to the ankles, the leather on the toe is stout and protective, and the soles are thick enough and strong enough to be good instruments. But for regular kicking over the long term, I've found hushpuppies to be about as good as any equipment, and wear them most of the time to be ready. The leather above the sole and around the toe is protective, the soles are thick enough, tough enough, and resilient enough for good work, and traction is good. Incidentally, I've not found much satisfaction in the precious new running shoes, jogging shoes, walking shoes, racquetballplaying shoes, drinking shoes, ironpumping shoes, and fornicating shoes now available at the precious new foot stores where the sales people dress like referees. Most of them don't give you that much protection up round your toes, and the cute way they have now of turning a little bitty part of the sole up at the toe means that you don't get a good flat surface for striking the rock. When the toe is turned up in that precious way, it means that you are often going to strike the rock just *under* your toe, and you can't count on much distance or accuracy that way, or much beauty in the kick.

The second necessary item of equipment is rocks, and that's been no problem that I can see. The world is a rock, and it is full of rocks. I prefer a rock no more than two inches across, and would usually choose rocks between ¾ and 1¼ inches, preferably a little rounded—the startlingly white, weather-smoothed granite pebbles that I know best in West Texas give great kicks. They are washed smooth by eons in some river, and hard enough to scratch glass. But after all, what one finally does may not depend upon choice at all—one kicks the rock that *must* be kicked.

Playing arenas are, so far, no problem, though as I suggested earlier, we could face some limitations if we continue to cover with concrete all of that part of the world where humans are. You need a good country lane once in a while, or a path, or a low, rolling hillside, or the floor of a canyon, or the rim of a canyon, or any place where rocks are abundant and you have choice. But you kick the rock that must be kicked, and a street or a sidewalk can give just as much pleasure—one way to get good evidence of your kick is to aim straight down a sidewalk. A flat, paved surface with few rocks can be a delight. Every Sunday morning I walk across campus to the local bookstore to get the *New York Times*. My route takes me across a large parking lot that's empty on Sunday mornings. It's pretty thrilling to come upon a good rock in that great open space, where the spaces marked off for cars give you yardmarkers, direction lines, and goals to aim at. It sometimes takes me a good while to get the Sunday paper.

But I said I'd come back to the rules of the sport. The rules, ladies and gentlemen, are none of your damned business. I want to celebrate the sport, but keep it in my mind. There's good reason why the literature of the sport is sparse: practitioners have chosen not to talk or to write save for few arcane texts, including those I mentioned earlier, and I rejoice now to concur in their silence. If we talk too much, if we explained all the rules and procedures, then you know what would happen. The sport would be professionalized and institutionalized. As Peter S. Wenz argues in "Human Equality in Sport," its exchange value would go up, its personal use value would go down, and worse would follow. Precious sweatsuits would be designed and produced and bought, then cute shorts. Darling sweat bands would be manufactured and marketed, and, Oh My God, the shoes—they'd design special shoes, and people would buy them.

Then they would have taken the sport away from me, as professionalization, institutionalization, age, and the lack of talent have taken all other sports away. Nothing much turned out the way I imagined it would. I guess I'm a little shocked, but not much surprised.

But for now, there's still rock-kicking. I won't tell you the rules and procedures. Some of you know them, and know the mysteries—how you know which pace, which foot, how you know when to start the walkup steps preparatory to kicking, how you know when it's going to go right. It's a game of the mind, and you must make the rules and imagine the procedures. You kick the rock that must be kicked, and you keep kicking and then you're free. The game can be played, preserved, cherished every day. I may just take the next championship; I'll for sure be in contention. It's held every day, and sometimes twice.

The Heroes Have Gone
From the Grocery Store

What I have to tell had its beginnings in a series of events in my freshman English class a few years ago. You have to understand that for close on to ten years I have been writing the essays that I assign to my freshman students, turning mine in to them as they turn theirs in to me.

I'd like for you to believe that what happened was in an appropriate context for the class. That, I suppose, is of no great moment to you, but matters considerably to me. At any rate, one morning in class I was playing my cello real hard, telling them that there was no such thing as a dull subject if you cared about writing, or about yourself. They reacted predictably enough, thought up four or five dull subjects, selected the one they thought was the worst, and challenged me to write my next essay on their dull subject. Their dull subject? A single Cheerio.

I put off writing the essay for a while, pretending that I was thinking it through. Finally I went to the grocery store just off campus, bought a box of Cheerios, and set out to work my way down to a single Cheerio. I studied the box and its insides, counted the Cheerios (there are about 2600, for the cynical among you), and selected the one I'd write about. But that's not part of my story. My story, for our present purposes, starts from what I saw when I studied the outside of the Cheerios box.

I'd like for you to know that, though I mostly believe in a breakfast made of pipe tobacco and coffee, I have spent my time, as three children grew up, in front of the grocery shelves where cereals are displayed. Selecting a cereal is not a casual art, and I have studied the craft, or so I thought.

My own pretensions to expertise notwithstanding, the Cheerios box brought me up short. (I want to report, before I go on, and you can trust me or not, as you please, that I was able finally to write a wonderfully adequate essay about a single Cheerio.) But what was on the outside of the box troubled me. Perhaps I'd never looked as closely as I had thought. Perhaps I hadn't paid enough attention over the years. What was there? The Hugga Bunch Kids—Hugsy and Impkins and Bubbles and Chumley and Huggins and Hugabye. ("Free inside, two Hugga Bunch Easy-Paint Postcards.")

I cannot account for what happened next. Perhaps it was a simple sequence of associations. Perhaps it wasn't simple. When you go back in me looking for something like the truth, sooner or later you come to abut the place of which there is no knowledge, whether that is prior to birth, in inadequate records, in mistaken memory or elsewhere. You come to abut that place in any search, if you go *back* in time, if you go *out* toward others, if you go *sideways* into your self in other manifestations or as perceived by others, if you go *down* into the subconscious, if you go *up* to wherever.

So, I don't know how to account for what happened next. When I saw the Hugga Bunch Kids on the Cheerios box, my mind went to Dizzy Dean and a Wheaties box, to the school year of 1937–1938 when I was in the second grade and started my baseball scrapbook, to the series that ran on the Wheaties boxes, "My Greatest Day in Sports." No trail of bread crumbs can be counted on to get you from the Hugga Bunch Kids to Dizzy Dean, but such transferences do occur, as you know well.

As I recall that particular series on the Wheaties boxes, it was a continuing account, by diverse sports figures, of their most thrilling day in sports. Charley Gehringer, the greatest second baseman, was also in the series, but it was Dizzy Dean who came to my mind, recalling as his greatest day the last game of the 1934 World Series, when the Cardinals beat the Detroit Tigers, 11–0, to take the championship. I cut out the story and picture for my scrapbook.

Suddenly, that day, I was startled by the change, on the back of cereal boxes, from Dizzy Dean to the Hugga Bunch Kids— Hugsy and Impkins and Bubbles and Chumley and Huggins and Hugabye. Dizzy would have thrown up.

So, startled, I did what I thought a scholar ought to do. I quit grading papers, quit doing whatever I was supposed to do, and went in search of information about this great cultural shift, from Dizzy Dean to the Hugga Bunch Kids. I set out to find traces of Dizzy Dean and all of the athletes who used to be on cereal boxes. I went looking for Wheaties boxes.

The library yielded James Gray's *Business Without Boundary, the Story of General Mills.* The first run of Wheaties was ready for the market in November 1924. Early on, Donald Davis insisted that the Washburn Crosby Company (as the company was then known) learn to use the new medium, radio, and by 1926, the first singing commercial was ready:

> Have you tried Wheaties?
> They're whole wheat with all of the bran.
> Won't you try Wheaties?
> For wheat is the best food of man.

After expanding sales with two radio programs, first "Skippy" then "Jack Armstrong," the company turned to a larger audience, began to sponsor baseball games on radio, and through Knox Reeves, one of the company's advertising agents, found its magic phrase, "Breakfast of Champions." Sales tripled during the depressed 1930s.

That's okay so far, I thought, but still no Dizzy Dean, no series called "My Greatest Day in Sports." I wrote to General Mills. A pleasant correspondence with Jean Toll, corporate archivist, followed. She was pleasant. What she taught me wasn't pleasant.

Her letter of April 28, 1987, brought me photocopies of various Wheaties package *fronts,* 1924–1976. Her letter of July 9, 1987, brought me word that she could not find the series I had asked about; with it were photocopies of two Wheaties backs, one from 1935 showing Dizzy Dean and his brother Daffy, hunkered down, examining a baseball, one from 1937 showing Joe DiMaggio stretched high to take a long fly, with the testimony, "Wheaties is just about the swellest dish I've ever eaten. A World Series thrill in breakfast enjoyment." Neither picture was accompanied by other text; there was no account of that 11-0 final game of the 1934 World Series. Her letter of August 5, 1987, brought more photocopies: from 1934, Jimmy Foxx, Ellsworth Vines, Jack Armstrong of Hudson High, Lou Gehrig, Chuck Klein, Mickey Cochran, Betty Fairfield (a golfer), Pepper Martin, Elinor Smith (a flier), Al Simmons, Wally Berger; from 1935, Bill Dickey, George Barclay (All-American guard from North Carolina), and the *Normandie*; from 1936, Jack Knaby (a flier), and Pepper Martin again.

"My Greatest Day in Sports" did not appear anywhere. There was no picture of Dizzy Dean with an account of that game, no picture of Charley Gehringer with an account of his greatest day. Ms. Toll said there had been no such series on Wheaties boxes.

I can still remember cutting out the back of that Wheaties box to put it in my scrapbook. Apparently the box I remember never existed.

Some time passed in depression before I could go on. Then I tried again. I didn't *always* eat Wheaties. From time to time I tried other cereals in those days. On July 29, 1987, I wrote to General Foods, thinking maybe the box and picture and text I remembered had been on Grape Nuts Flakes, or maybe Post Bran Flakes, or maybe even Post Toasties, though God knows they turned soggy the moment you put milk on them. I've had no answer from General Foods. I don't believe they're going to write.

I mostly know what's on cereal boxes now, but I can't find Dizzy Dean and the text of that 1934 most-thrilling day. Wheaties has Chris Evert (the large box has Walter Payton). Total has Angela Lansbury's Mystery Sweepstakes, featuring the "Mystery of the Missing Vitamins." Captain Crunch has the Captain and a bunch of kids marveling over the spinning globes to be found inside the box. Shredded Wheat has a wonderful diagram of a wheat kernel and a recipe. Trix has a connect-the-dots puzzle called "Who gummed up the Trix machine?" Fruit Loops has a color-by-number picture of protoceratops. Corn Chex, for God's sake, has instructions about how kids can fly free on Piedmont. Cocoa Pebbles has instructions about how to get private eye glasses like Fred Flintstone and Barney Rubble wear. I can't go on. I mostly know what's on the boxes now.

But I can't find Dizzy's text. These days, it's hard to find a text under any circumstances. Does it exist on the page or in the speech? Does it exist only in reader's or a hearer's interpretation? Do I grow fuzzy around the edges and blur before your eyes? Do I disappear even while I speak, as you interpret—or ignore—what I say? Have I gone altogether? I know that Dizzy Dean did, in fact, pitch a six-hit shutout that time in the 1934 World Series, that the game was never in doubt after the third inning. But I can't find the Wheaties box, or his text. Perhaps it's no matter. Ole Diz didn't write it, anyway.

The catch is, I *thought* he did. The catch is, I *thought* I had a text of sports. It came from John Tunis and from piles of pulp magazines. It came from Ralph Henry Barbour and all those books about the wonderful lads at Yardley High and from Wheaties boxes. It came from Jayton High School, in West Texas, where I grew part way up—and I didn't even get that part right. For years, I've told my children and anyone else who would listen about my brave older brother, and how he was starting guard when he was just a 135 pound sophomore. He wasn't. I learned lately from microfilms of the weekly newspaper in Jayton, that he was a substitute, just a substitute. And my sports text came, too, from TCU, in 1938, when the Horned Frogs were national champions and Davey O'Brien and Ki Aldrich were more than a boy could imagine. I first learned about universities by listening to Saturday afternoon games in 1938, the first year I was much acquainted with radios. TCU beat Centenary 13–10, then Arkansas, 21–14. Then they played Temple and won 28–6. Next was A&M, and the headline said, "Frogs Smash Aggies, 21–6! Aldrich, O'Brien Star." Then they beat Marquette, 21–0, and Baylor, 39–7, and Tulsa, 21–0.

The headline on Sunday, November 12, said "O'Brien's Passes Sink Texas, 28–6." Then they won over Rice by 29 to 7. Finally the headline for November 26 said, "Frogs Use Power to Beat Ponies, 20–7, for Conference Title." A little later they played Carnegie Tech in the Sugar Bowl and won 15–7.

The catch is, I thought Dizzy Dean wrote that text that I can't find. The catch is, I thought the lads all went out for football *after* they arrived at the university. The catch is, I thought I had a sports text. I kept telling myself stories. Peter Brooks remarks in *Reading for the Plot* that "our lives are ceaselessly intertwined with narrative, with the stories that we tell and hear told, those we dream or imagine or would like to tell, all of which are reworked in that story of our own lives that we narrate to ourselves in an episodic, sometimes semiconscious, but virtually uninterrupted monologue." I told myself stories, and thought I had a sports text.

But much that I saw and thought, I saw and thought wrong, and then misremembered. Most things, I never saw at all. I took as mine a vision that is or was, as Gary Wills put it in *Reagan's America*, "beyond or below ideology," a vision that comes from America's past, but doesn't reflect reality at all. Parts of it never did, and other parts no longer do. Reluctant as I am to call up such company, I've joined the fellow in the White House and thousands of my countrymen in what I didn't yet know was pretense and self-deception, mistakenly enacting again a peculiarly American form of the idea of innocence, invoking again and again, as Stanley Hoffman put it in his review (May

28, 1987 *New York Review of Books*) of Wills's book,

> the cult of the individual acting without any
> "need for historical process, social transaction,
> political pressures, the play of interests," the
> myth of the small town as the locus of purity
> and simplicity the celebration of sports "as a
> moral paradigm for the young," where "inno-
> cence and aspiration verge on the religious,"
> the conviction that evil can only come from
> the outside . . . .

These myths, I come lately to find, may only be defense against
some reality that I haven't been able to deal with—say the reality of my own mistakenness, or the reality of a capitalism and a
technology that render the individual powerless, except if he is
a thief or a terrorist or a lawyer or a Wall Street broker.

You see, I thought it was all the way it is in Roy Stokes's book,
Andy at Yale, published in 1914. I thought pitchers were pure
and intense. I thought the lads went out for football *after* they
arrived at the university. My sports text was wrong. I didn't get
most of it right the first time, and then I misremembered what
I had misunderstood. Now it's gone. I can't find the Wheaties
box that I was looking for. My sports text won't recreate itself,
and I've come to know that if your heroes aren't regenerative,
you're lonesome when they die.

Some time ago I read in the newspaper that Ken Maynard

had died. The news brought on another considerable depression. I felt so low that I had to refrain from grading papers. Lou Gehrig was long since dead. Babe Ruth was long since dead, and so was Charley Gehringer, and so was Honus Wagner, and so was Tris Speaker, and so was Christy Mathewson. Franklin D. Roosevelt was long since dead, and when you get to be fifteen before you realize that anyone else can be president, then the rest sort of seem like imposters. And now, the last of the Big Five was dead.

Tom Mix died in 1940 in a car wreck. Buck Jones died in 1942 in the terrible fire at the Coconut Grove. Hoot Gibson died in 1966 of cancer. I don't know what happened to Hopalong Cassidy, but he's gone. And now Ken Maynard was dead at 77. He made 300 western movies and sometimes in the 1930s earned as much a $8000 a week. But he died in a small house trailer, alone, of physical deterioration and malnutrition. And all those others died, and the list is long, so long.

Mickey Mantle, August 10, 1995

The paper says that good old Mick is ill,
is dying, does not note that I am dying, too, though I was always slower than he
at nearly everything. We came along
together, but I bet he doesn't know.

I learned about him first in Germany,
in fifty-one, cold fall. We sat
around a fuel stove, our back sides chilled,
to hear the rookie's narrative, just come to
his first Series play. the game came out of air
long after it was over, came to our tent
and army radio in scary dark
and hurting cold. We waited after midnight, heard the ump call out "Play ball,"

and followed every out and run.

I saw him later frequently in TV games.
I saw him bounce a drive against the roof —
you know, the second deck. The ball was still,
they say, upon its upward flight. I saw
him, loping toward the wall, take in a fly
where others would have run full out and
missed, and saw him put sweet bunts down
                                    either line.
When the camera came in close to him at bat,
I heard old Dizzy say, "Just look at him —
he's squeezing saw dust outta that stick,
and that poor pitcher, he ain't got a chance."
Old Dizzy didn't favor batters much.

I guess he was a drunk, perhaps a lout,
but he was good, and he is dying now.
We came along together. Now I'm left,
and I can't fill the world the way he could,
can't get to first as fast, or make it home.

World War II on Cleckler Street

Perhaps if I had lived at another place in a different time when I was eleven and twelve and thirteen, I would have been busy plowing, or dying, or studying Latin and Greek. As it was in Fort Worth, Texas, on Cleckler Street in 1941, 1942, and 1943, my time was pretty well used up with throwing newspapers on my route, hanging around, playing ball, reading books, trying to build model airplanes, and swapping comic books, chiefly with George Weatherly and R. L. Anderson. R. L.'s name was Raymond Lewis, but no one called him that.

I didn't then and don't now know just how swapping succeeded as it did. Both George and R. L. were good at it, though George was the real expert. I don't remember ever actually buying comic books, and I don't remember actually seeing them buy comic books, but somehow comic books accumulated. Probably one reason I enjoyed swapping with them was that I liked their style, which pretty much coincided with mine. They didn't want to swap one or two comic books at a time. They waited until a bunch had accumulated, maybe a five or six or ten-inch stack. Then you really had something to look at.

Comic books about cartoon characters—Donald Duck and the others—I didn't care for much, so I got through them pretty fast. I still haven't figured out what distinguishes a cartoon character, say Porky Pig, from a cartoon character, say the Shadow, but the distinction was real enough in my head.

Super heroes like Captain Marvel were better, but still not my favorites, so those comic books didn't take too long, either. But when it came to Batman and the Green Lantern, and later, Blackhawk, that was a different matter. Those comic books warranted slow, careful scrutiny.

And then I discovered *Wings Comics*. Ah, *Wings Comics*.

I was already missing the comic strip fliers I had learned about earlier, especially Tailspin Tommy and Scorchy Smith. I didn't know then whether I had disappeared to them (in the late 1930s and early 1940s my family didn't always get newspapers), or they had disappeared to me as strips ceased publication. Later, Ron Goulart notified me, in *The Adventurous Decade*, that "*Tailspin Tommy* faded out and disappeared from the comic pages about the time the United States entered the Second World War. Biplanes and barnstormers didn't mean much anymore." I didn't for a while know exactly what happened to *Scorchy Smith*, which I saw infrequently. The strip began in 1930 at the hand of John Terry. By late 1933, Noel Sickles was drawing the strip, developing the "impressionistic, lushly black style which his friend Milton Caniff later appropriated for *Terry and the Pirates*." When John Terry died in 1934, Sickles was free to sign his own name to the strip, but he was tired of it by the end of 1936, and Allan Christman, a youngster of twenty, began drawing it. After about a year and a half, Christman went on to other things, but not for long. Scorchy Smith was still being published, I thought, as late as 1939, but Goulart suggests that neither Scorchy nor Allan Christman could last long. Christman trained as a navy fly cadet, then joined Chennault's Flying Tigers in China. On his third mission, on January 23, 1942, he bailed out of his crippled P40. Goulart reports that "a Japanese plane went after him and machine-gunned him. Christman, twenty-six now, was dead before he hit the ground." That, of course, would be difficult to verify, but what I said a moment ago was simply wrong. *Scorchy Smith* survived with a variety of artists and writers until 1960. Perhaps Goulart was right when he suggested that after January 23, 1942, it was a new world, "no place for the grinning, slightly innocent air daredevils. There would be more fliers in the comic pages as the Second World War went on. But they were warriors, not soldiers-of-fortune. That had ended." I mostly doubt that there were any soldiers-of-fortune like Scorchy Smith. I expect that if I had met a soldier-of-fortune, I wouldn't have liked what I saw.

For a little while at least, I guess the war put an end to the possibility of being a soldier-of-fortune as a career choice. By 1942, the fliers were mostly military people, and so I came to know *Wings Comics*. Don Thompson and Dick Lupoff, in *The Comic Book Book*, report that the first issue of *Wings Comics* was dated September 1940. By that time, of course, there were gallant young men in Spitfires and Hurricanes to celebrate. I think it must have been 1943 before I encountered the comic book.

I was drawn to *Wings Comics* first by the airplanes. They were generally recognizable, though not always well-drawn and seldom detailed.

But oh my, there were other reasons to notice *Wings Comics*, more, it seemed, with each issue, other reasons than airplanes to save *Wings* for last and best.

Women.

With each new issue, there were more women, or at least the possibility that there might be more women, and with each new issue each of them might show more of herself to us. Might happen, you know. Do you wish to contemplate the exact difference between one cartoon character, say Daffy Duck, and another cartoon character, say a nude Air Corps nurse, ever so dimly suggested behind a shower curtain? Maybe it matters how old you are when you encounter each.

The increasing incidence of what some are pleased to call "scantily-clad women" was not, of course, confined to *Wings Comics*. As William Savage reported in *Comic Books in America, 1945–1954*:

> The war changed the appearance of comic books, probably because so many servicemen read them. By 1945, their artwork developed a sexual orientation remarkable in a medium ostensibly still intended for juvenile audiences. A typical wartime cover might reveal in the foreground a scantily clad woman, tied with ropes or chains, at the mercy of a leering Axis villain, while in the background an American hero struggled forward, intent upon her rescue. The woman's clothing inevitably was torn to reveal ample cleavage and thigh, her muscular definition enhanced by forced contortion into some anatomically impossible position. Sometimes, her clothing was completely ripped away, leaving her to face her

tormentor clad only in her unmentionables—
which, presumably, gave added incentive to
the struggling hero back there. The stories
inside rarely if ever fulfilled the promises of
such a cover, but they usually paid sufficient
attention to female secondary sex character-
istics to warrant a fellow's perusal.

But in 1943, if that's when it was, *Wings Comics* was my most reliable source on women, reason enough to save it for last when
I had swapped for a new stack of comic books. Thompson and
Lupoff provide some particulars in their account of an episode
featuring Frisco Flo:

Flo is a breathtaking siren. Her auburn-rich
red hair flows to her shoulders in sensuous-
looking waves; she wears a floor-length yellow dress cut all the way to the sternum at the
top and slashed well up to the thigh at the
bottom. The artist . . . lovingly shades every
line and curve of Flo's generous bosom and
graceful hips. She stands usually with one
hand on her hip and her dress clings so that
even her navel is clearly delineated!

In the particular episode at issue, Flo has the secret location of
West Coast arsenals tattooed in code on her thigh, "providing

the artist an excuse for three more luscious garter shots."

In 1943, when you're twelve going on thirteen, it doesn't get any better than that.

Since, I have often wondered what unexpected sources shaped my expectations, my ways of thinking. Was *Wings Comics* one of the influential textbooks of my life? Because of that text, did I get some things wrong almost from the start? Of course, other sources were available in those years, even on Cleckler Street. I waited for my brother, but there wasn't much chance to learn a lot from him, though I did pick up what I was pretty sure were valuable secrets from him about how to handle a gun turret on a B24. Still, his leave time from the Air Corps was scant, and I had to turn elsewhere for full-time tutelage.

As the war went on and I turned fourteen and fifteen, I came to read the newspapers more and more faithfully, and was soon addicted to *Life* and *Look* and then to *Time.* All brought us simple messages, as Savage notes of comic books:

> Comic books brought much to the American cause. In addition to lending support to such necessary activities as bond drives and paper drives, comic books became an integral part of the Allied propaganda machine war effort by portraying the enemy as the inhuman offspring of a vast and pernicious evil. Writers coined epithets like "ratzi" and "Japanazi," and artists drew rodentlike Japanese and

bloated, sneering Germans. Japanese troops wore thick glasses and displayed prominent teeth, while German officers possessed monocles and dueling scars, much as they did in the wartime renditions of Hollywood filmmakers—although comic book illustrators took greater liberties than Hollywood could, and to great effect, given the nature of caricature.

All of them told us what they thought we needed to know, and when I look back now, I don't think *Life* and *Look* and *Time* were much more reliable than the comic books.

Or the movies.

I was just about as late coming to movies for my education as I was to comic books. Before, we had lived in rural territory where movies weren't available, and when my family first moved to the city, money wasn't available. But by 1942, I had a paper route, I usually had a couple of quarters I could rub together in my pocket, and a splendor was close by, admission only a dime. About four blocks south of our house, Cleckler Street came to a dead end at Belknap Street. Just around the corner was the Tower Theater, a brandnew neighborhood movie palace.

When you're twelve going on thirteen, it doesn't get any better than that. When I look back, I think life must have been pretty slow and sweet and easy for me on Cleckler Street. In my memory, it's always summer there, and the street is mostly in the shade. Throwing papers on my route in the morning was all right—when I was done, I could go home and sleep some more. In the afternoon, I'd get pretty hot, but about halfway through my route there was a filling station where I could stop, lift the lid of the soft drink box out front, and fish out a cold Barq's Root Beer that still cost a nickel. Afterward,

maybe there'd be a ball game, or a movie. The Tower Theater showed three different movies a week, as most theaters did. As I recall, a big movie played on Sunday, Monday, and Tuesday, a "B" movie on Wednesday and Thursday, and another big one on Friday and Saturday. I had plenty of chances to learn about the war at the Tower Theater. I might have learned more and better elsewhere, I expect.

I waited for my brother to come home, but he wouldn't come back until 1945, and he was married, anyway, and didn't really come home. In a front window at our house, my mother had put a little flag. It was maybe seven inches wide and ten inches long, and it hung vertically in the window. It had a red border and a white field. On the white field, there was a blue star for my brother. Other houses close by on Cleckler Street had flags, too. One had two blue stars for two members of the family who were away in the service. At one house, the flag in the window had a gold star. Whoever left that house for military service had been killed. I might have learned more and better elsewhere, I expect, but I mostly learned about the war down at the Tower Theater.

That's where I learned how things were supposed to be. That's where I learned how we fought wars. I saw *Bataan* and *Wake Island* and *Gung Ho!* I saw *Bombardier* and *Air Force* and *Captains of the Clouds* and *A Yank in the RAF.* I saw *Crash Dive* and *Cry Havoc* and *The Purple Heart* and *Guadalcanal Diary* and *So Proudly We Hail* and *Dive Bomber* and *Eagle Squadron* and *The Edge of Darkness* and *The Halls of Montezuma* and *Pin Up Girl* and

Sahara and *A Walk in the Sun*. God knows what else I saw.

I came to know that our lads who fought were decent and skilled, that our bomber pilots always flew true courses, that our bombardiers always hit military precisely. I heard wonderful stories about our fliers' precision, about, for example, the RAF Mosquito pilot, who, flying in at rooftop level, put a bomb through the exact building that was his target. I came to know things, as Alvin H. Rosenfeld puts it in *Imagining*, pretty much as others knew them,

> for most people do not have a primary relationship with "the facts" and learn about them secondhand, through the mediations of word and image. With few exceptions we "see" what we are given to see, "know" what we given to know, and thus come to retain in memory what impresses itself on us as vision and knowledge.

Imagine my surprise when, much later, I began to learn that it was usually otherwise. *Life* and *Look* and *Time* and the movies turned out to be scarcely more reliable than books. Imagine my surprise when I began, much later, to learn that our bombers were not exact in their aim. Imagine my surprise when I began to learn that we had deliberately bombed civilians.

A pamphlet published in 1942 describes the "weapon of ultimate victory," the B17 Flying Fortress, "the mightiest bomber ever built." It is described as a precision instrument, "equipped with the incredibly accurate Norden bomb sight which hits a 25-foot circle from 20,000 feet." The pamphlet argues that the B17 is especially safe for its crewmen because, given the accuracy of the bomb sight, it can fly higher than the range of anti-aircraft guns. And yet 22,000 of them went down on the fields of war, carrying about 110,000 airmen. Bombing turned out to be so inaccurate that the planes had to fly well within the range of anti-aircraft fire. Early in the war, the RAF Bomber Command assumed that only one in ten of its bombers would get within five miles of the assigned target.

Paul Fussell details episodes of inaccuracy in *Wartime*. In May 1940, a Luftwaffe squadron set out to bomb Dijon, but instead dropped its bombs on German civilians in Freiburg. The Germans handled this nicely: it was the British or the French, they said, who dropped the bombs; everyone knows that bombers are accurate. In July 1944, ground forces were stopped near the Normandy beach-head at St. Lo. Operation COBRA was designed to break them loose.

Some 1,800 bombers were to devastate the German defenders on July 25, so that the Allied ground forces could move on. Because of a communications mistake, many planes dropped their bombs on the day before, and so inaccurately that twenty-five American soldiers were killed and 131 were wounded. The operation was resumed the next day. The American line had been secretly withdrawn thousands of yards to avoid being bombed again. This time, the bombs killed 111 Americans and wounded about 500. It was the inaccuracy of the bombers that had led, early in the war, to the practice of "area bombing."

But I didn't learn that until much later. *Life* and *Look* and *Time* and the movies and comic books didn't tell me. They didn't tell us what they thought we didn't need to know. In 1945, 1 still believed that Allied bombardiers could place their bombs exactly where they wanted them, on military targets and war industries. I believed that until 1951, when I was stationed in Germany and saw Mannheim and Frankfurt, still mostly ruin and rubble, and still half believed until I read Sir Arthur Harris' directive of February 1942, to the RAF Bomber

Command: "the primary object of your operation should now be focused on the morale of the enemy civilian population." And they didn't tell us, as Fussell also reports, about the casualties off Slapton Sands in the practice invasion preparatory to the Normandy landing. Nine German U-boats got in among the practice invasion fleet, sinking landing craft and drowning 750 soldiers and sailors. Their deaths were listed among the casualties of the Normandy invasion.

And they didn't tell us what they apparently didn't know, though they could have known if they had investigated. We didn't begin to see the ghostly remnants of the Holocaust until 1945.

My sources, it turns out, were not reliable.

I don't long to recapture that old vision of how things were supposed to be. I mostly had things wrong. I regret that I didn't know more and otherwise sooner. I regret that we couldn't take ourselves as we were. I regret that I was ever proud of bombardiers. I regret that I was ever attracted by war stories. I know that it's not unusual. Only a little while ago, someone called the conflict in the Persian Gulf "a magnificent war," and thousands waved or wore yellow ribbons to glorify it all.

I regret that I was ever attracted by war stories, and yet I have turned back, time and again, and not so long ago, to accounts of the Battle of Verdun. Commencing on February 21, 1916, French and German troops fought over and for an area smaller than Manhattan. About 420,000 were killed. I have turned back, time and again, to accounts of that battle, wondering whether or not I could have measured up to that hellish testing.

Well, no more. On Cleckler Street, I was sorry that I wasn't old enough to go to war. It didn't seem right that others had to go while I stayed, safe and cool in the shade on Cleckler Street. I regret that I was ever attracted by war stories, and I regret that I ever thought war to be the appropriate test for manhood.

But it's not easy to give up your war stories; it entails regretting your life.

I haven't lived on Cleckler Street for forty-seven years, and yet I still live on Cleckler Street. Somewhere back there I learned what it is to be a man, or so I thought. I've spent a good part of my adult life trying to learn what it was I thought I learned early, who or what taught me, and where those notions originated. Sometimes now, when my wife thinks some attitude I've articulated is weird, when she asks me where such ideas come from, all I can do is say, "It's the Code of the West, Ma'am." That's not an answer, but often it's the only answer I have.

I learned from my father and my brother and my friends that the first essential requirement for manhood is physical strength, together with physical dexterity, agility, even grace. I don't know whether or not they actually believed it. This physical mastery was supposed to manifest itself wherever needed, whether it was in defending a lady; in lifting 100pound sacks of cow feed; in driving fast with one hand on the steering wheel, the other arm draped over the open window; in fighting over an affront, whether real or imagined, to one's honor; or in dropping a forty-yard pass right over the shoulder of a receiver running full out down the sideline. I never measured up in this respect, and I've always been embarrassed about that.

I learned on Cleckler Street or somewhere that, to be a man, you're supposed to be stoical in the face of pain, unweeping in the face of grief. I never measured up in this respect, and I've always been embarrassed about that.

From my brother, the sports pages, diverse coaches, the sports fiction I read, from *Andy at Yale*, the first book I ever owned, and who knows where else, I learned that to be a real man, you had to prove yourself, and I learned that the second best place to do that was in athletic competition. I never measured up in this respect, and I've always been embarrassed about that.

From comic books and *Life* and *Look* and *Time* and the movies, and from other lies I heard and read on Cleckler Street, I learned that the best place to prove yourself a man was in war. I never measured up in this respect, and I've always been embarrassed about that.

I've often wondered whether, if you are conditioned to think in certain ways and you know that you are conditioned, but you still think in those ways, then are you still conditioned? I don't know.

I do know that it's hard to change some habits of behavior and thought.

But I'm going to try. I'm not going to study war anymore. Or competition. Or manhood defined in those old terms. I may not make it.

I guess it's easy for me to say that I'll study war no more. It's unlikely that I'll be in danger. I'll not be asked to serve, and probably won't be asked to prove myself.

But it's not easy for me to think such thoughts. It's like surrendering a lifetime of thinking. That's not easy, I judge, either for my country or for me. Along about May, 1990, for fifteen or twenty minutes, it looked as if we all might have grown up enough to follow peaceful paths. Didn't turn out that way. In January of 1991 we went to war again. For about ten minutes, I thought perhaps at least we'd grown up enough to be told the truth about war and our participation in it. Didn't turn out that way. The television news and the speeches and the magazines were just about as evasive as the movie and comic book and magazine versions of World War II. For about five minutes on Friday, January 18, 1991, I caught myself being proud about our side's skill in precision bombing. I don't want to think such thoughts anymore.

Sometimes, when I passed the house on Cleckler Street where there was a gold star on the little flag, I was taken by stillness. Sometimes, I'd guess, I didn't notice. So many died. One was from Cleckler Street. But life for me, I think, was sweet and slow and easy.

I'll remember Cleckler Street. It's always summer there. The trees are green. The street is quiet in the blue shade. Moments of sunlight dance through the leaves and touch the street. After I had finished my afternoon route, sometimes there was a ball game. When the other team made its third out and we came in to bat, sometimes somebody would say, "Okay—everybody bats this time. Everybody bats." And then maybe some others would take it up and chant, "Everybody bats. Everybody bats." I wish we'd known to say more. I wish we'd known to say, "Everybody bats, and no one dies. No one dies. No one dies."

Making Las Vegas

When problems and puzzles persist, and not only persist, but catch my attention fully and engage me, I usually indulge in the continuing hope that if I just knew enough, if I would just study far enough, if I would just work hard enough, eventually there'd be a completely satisfying resolution, and I would have the truth. What was Jayton really like in 1938? What became of the people in Fluvanna and Clairmont and Kalgary and Peacock? Exactly where is Oriana? How did Las Vegas become a place for me? If I knew enough, if I studied far enough, if I worked hard enough, then I would know and have the truth. That is not going to happen. I won't have the truth.

In most of our large and small enterprises, we have to make do without expertise. That isn't a reason to recommend indifference to study, but the world usually won't wait until we get ready. Jobs and flower beds and making scones use up the time, and if in my mind I have little time, I mostly have less patience. I don't know the truth about Jayton or Aspermont or Spur or Fluvanna, either, and I doubt that I'll ever learn exactly how and why Las Vegas came to be a place for me. That puzzle may even have a simple solution, but I don't imagine I'll be able to feel sure about it, even if that is the case. I won't be able to learn enough. It's an interesting, sometimes sad, sometimes exciting predicament, dramatized in a metaphor used by David Lowenthal and others, taking the self as an island. If as an infant or child one may be taken as a small island, then the boundaries to the unknown are small. If the island, then, may be allowed to grow as a person acquires knowledge, its boundaries to the unknown are larger.

I doubt, then, that I'll be either able or willing to learn all that might be learned from urbanists, architects, geographers, and landscape historians.

Sometimes I accompany my wife when she goes to professional conferences. She is customarily busy all day, and my custom is to walk for hours each day wherever we are, seeing new territory or seeing familiar territory for the first time. We go each fall to Chicago and, because of the location of the meeting, stay at one or another hotel near the intersection of Ohio Street and Michigan Avenue, which means that I can walk throughout the Loop and the near North Side, and could go farther if my knees would hold out. A couple of years ago, I went with her to a small conference in Houston. Houston has not just one high-rise skyline, but several. Our hotel was in one of the other big cities contained in Houston, not downtown, not where major shopping and eating facilities are located, but a big city of office buildings and hotels. On our first morning there, I went out of the hotel's front entrance and discovered that there was no place to walk. I hadn't realized it when we had driven in the previous evening, but we were in a concrete and glass compound. In front of me and the hotel was a major freeway, beyond it a large construction project. To my right was another major freeway, across it only anonymous office buildings. To my left stretched a double row of concrete and glass office buildings that formed the rest of our compound. Behind me and the hotel, I learned shortly, was a high wall that separated the hotel and the office buildings from a major street. There was no place for me to get. To go for a walk and to be able to see things, I'd have to get the car out and drive somewhere. I went back inside and read until the bar on the top floor of the hotel opened. From there, I could see the compound. Looking out, I began to understand, in a baffled and bemused sort of way, Robert Riley's observation that ours are "diverse landscapes created and used by voluntary specialinterest groups, each with its own ways of shaping, using, selling, and perceiving the environment." He discusses as samples some new subcultural landscapes, some new urban landscapes, some landscapes of nostalgia, and some packaged landscapes. I understood about the last pretty quickly: I was in one.

I begin, too, I think, to understand Pierce F. Lewis' reminder that landscape is not pretty scenes but all that we see outside:

It rarely occurs to most Americans to think of landscape as including everything from city skylines to farmers' silos, from golf courses to garbage dumps, from ski slopes to manure piles, from millionaires' mansions to the tract houses of Levittown, from famous historical landmarks to flashing electric signs that boast the creation of the 20 billionth hamburger, from mossy cemeteries to sleazy shops that sell pornography next door to big city bus stations— in fact, whole countrysides, and whole cities, whether ugly or beautiful makes no difference.

All of the human landscape has cultural meaning, Lewis says, and we can learn to read this landscape to learn what we are like, treating most items in the language as "no more and no less important than other times." If Louis Sullivan's buildings are revelatory, so, too, are casino signs in Las Vegas:

Our human landscape is our unwitting autobiography, reflecting our tastes, our values, our aspirations, and even our fears, in tangible, visible form. We rarely think of landscape that way, and so the cultural record we have "written" in the landscape is liable to

be more truthful than most autobiographies
because we are less selfconscious about how
we describe ourselves.

In *Closeup: How to Read the American City,* Grady Clay remarks
that "there are no secrets in the landscape." Our warts and
blemishes are there, Lewis says, and "our glories too; but above
all, our ordinary day-to-day qualities are exhibited for anybody
who wants to find them and knows how to look for them."

I don't. I can't read Las Vegas in the ways that Lewis (and
others) suggest. Such a reading would entail knowing when
and why pressures for change have been exerted, when and
where and why regional variations persist or disappear in the
city, would entail knowing when and how and why the scene
converges with scenes elsewhere, would entail knowing when
and how and why imitation occurs and which way it flows, would
entail knowing not just the look of the casinos and hotels, but
also the look of motels, gas stations, shopping centers and
strips, billboards, homes, mobile homes, churches, water tow-
ers, city dumps, and so on, would entail knowing when tools
and technologies were available, would entail knowing the
physical, geographical context. I won't know Las Vegas as Lewis
and others suggest, and I won't see it and understand it as neu-
roscientists and perceptual psychologists might teach me. I do
know that on the first visit to Las Vegas, and sometimes thereafter, I was confused because sensory information was coming
toward me much faster that I could make sense of it. Lewis

does acknowledge that sometimes the landscape doesn't speak to us very clearly. Sometimes, it scarcely speaks to me at all.

When I look at Las Vegas, sometimes all I can hear or read is my history, and so my ability to read the city is bound by my own dimensions. Stanley Paher's *Las Vegas, As It Began—As It Grew* tells a history, but it begins with travelers in the area before 1848, and devotes only a little of its last chapter to reasonably contemporary Las Vegas. Histories are missing. Tom Wolfe says, in *The Kandy-Kolored Tangerine-Flake Streamline Baby*, that

> . . . Las Vegas is the only town in the world whose skyline is made up neither of buildings, like New York, nor of trees, like Wilbraham, Massachusetts, but signs. One can look at Las Vegas from a mile away on Route 91 and see no buildings, no trees, only signs. But such signs! They tower. They revolve, they oscillate, they soar in shapes before which the existing vocabulary of art history is helpless. I can only attempt to supply names—Boomerang Modem, Palette Curvilinear, Flash Gordon MingAlert Spiral, McDonald's Hamburger Parabola, Mint Casino Elliptical, Miami Beach Kidney.

But the signs do signal. They situate entities—casinos, hotels, places—for which I have no history.

Some restrictions on gambling were established with the formation of the Nevada Territory, but when Nevada became a state in 1864, the legislature eased the restrictions to treat gambling as a misdemeanor. In 1869, gambling was legalized. Las Vegas was formed in 1905. The railroad that would be Union Pacific sold lots in what would become the downtown area of the city. In 1909, the state prohibited all forms of gambling.

Gambling was now a felony. In 1928, President Coolidge signed the Boulder Dam Act, appropriating $165 million for the construction. In 1930 Boulder Dam was renamed Hoover Dam. In 1931, all forms of gambling were legalized, and quick divorces were legalized in Las Vegas. President Roosevelt dedicated the dam in 1935, changing the name back to Boulder Dam. In 1945, control of gambling was shifted from local county control to the state for purposes of tax collection. In 1946, the Flamingo opened. Congress changed the name back to Hoover Dam in 1947, and in 1948 the new McCarran airport was dedicated. In 1949, new legislation made it possible for the tax commission to investigate the background of anyone applying for a gambling license. In 1959, the State Gaming Control Board was established. In 1963, the new McCarran International Airport was opened. In 1966, Caesar's Palace opened. During the years 1967–1969, Howard Hughes, who was living in the Desert Inn, bought the Desert Inn, the Sands, the Castaways, the Frontier, the Silver Slipper, and the Landmark, some of which were later sold by the Hughes Company. Some thought that Hughes' actions were a major factor in changing Las Vegas' image from that of a city of mob gamblers to that of a city of corporate gamblers. In 1986, Bally, the slot machine manufacturer, bought the MGM Grand. In 1988–1989, Mirage and Excalibur opened, and MGM announced plans for a huge new resort. In 1993, Luxor, Treasure Island, and the MGM opened.

In 1990, I went with my wife—she'd been there before—on my first trip to Las Vegas and began creating the city's history.

It was an alien place, and it remained alien until I created Las Vegas in my mind.

I have no other history. I won't be able to learn all that those others know. Even if I knew enough, studied far enough, worked hard enough, I'd still not be able to see and to think and to know as those others do.

Still, I can begin to make a little sense of what happened to me in Las Vegas, of what happened to Las Vegas in me.

I can begin to make a little sense of how I learned and played and created Las Vegas. Her ways are different, delightful, instructive. "As every personal history results in a particular private milieu," David Lowenthal says, "no one can ever duplicate the *terra cognita* of anyone else."

At first, and sometimes thereafter, I was confused and addled, displaced, unsituated. I knew a lady once who seemed to take all of earth as home, who seemed to be at home in any place. After all of these years, I begin to learn that I can't do that. In one way or another, I have to get myself situated, have to find some home base, before I can begin to make sense of new experiences and new places, and even then, what I learn is limited.

I wonder about how others manage. If you're already at home wherever you go, like the lady I knew, then is every place you go already familiar? If every place is already familiar, then why would you have any need to learn each new place? Her way, I expect, is better than mine, but from the place where I am, I can't entirely understand it. How can those we call homeless ever be found? How do those who do not start from places think? Why do I have to get situated? Placed? Should I learn at last that I am perpetually uprooted, as perhaps we all are, and so go looking always for some little staying place, here, there, or yonder?

I don't know. She is eager for experience and does not want to miss anything. She goes into experience much faster than I do, but I surely enjoy watching, even when I'm otherwise addled and displaced.

Venturi, Brown, and Izenour, the authors of *Learning from Las Vegas*, remark that in Las Vegas, "complex programs and settings require complex combinations of media beyond the purer architectural triad of structure, form, and light at the service of space. They suggest an architecture of bold communication rather than one of subtle expression." Most things along the Strip are not permanent, including myself. The extraordinary signs, I gather, have about the same life expectancy as an automobile. As Venturi, Brown, and Izenour point out, a single postcard can carry a view of the heart of downtown gambling, but the spaces of the Strip, they say, "must be seen as moving sequences." The Dunes sign, for example, now long gone, was two-dimensional, its front and back identical, but it was "an erection 22 stories high that pulsates at night." Where the signs are not solely perpendicular to the road, they are big enough, long enough, spectacular enough to be seen by moving observers, as is the case with the great, gaudy sign that stretches along most of the front of the Flamingo Hilton. And even if the pilgrim misses the signs, he or she can scarcely miss the fairy castle that is Excalibur, the pyramid of Luxor, or the great lion of the MGM Grand. The pilgrim's way is not stopped except by traffic lights, and hotel lobbies and casinos are open to the "Promenading public," and the pilgrim's way always leads to gambling spaces, always at the front. Typically, the pilgrim progresses from gambling areas to dining, entertainment, and shopping areas, then to the hotel. The gambling room is typically dark, and it has no windows: The combination of darkness and enclosure of the gambling room and its subspaces makes for privacy, protection, concentration, and control. The intricate maze under the low ceiling never connects with outside light or outside space. This disorients the occupant in space and time. One loses track of where one is and when it is. Time is limitless, because the light of noon and midnight are exactly the same. Space is limitless, because the artificial light obscures rather than defines its boundaries. Light is not used to define space. Walls and ceilings do not serve as reflective surfaces for light but are made absorbent and dark. Space is enclosed but limitless, because its edges are dark. The casino in Las Vegas, Venturi, Brown, and Izenour say, is a big, low space, "the archetype for all public interior spaces whose heights are diminished for reasons of budget and air conditioning."

Say if it pleases you that the Strip is gaudy, garish, awful, and artificial, but recognize, too, that its creators designed what they wanted, and their designs work as they wanted them to work.

But I didn't think about such things at first, and have only infrequently thought about such things since. I haven't learned, and probably won't, about tribes, cultures, subcultures, histories, flora, fauna, topography, ethnography of Las Vegas. The jumbled images that were my first impressions of Las Vegas sometimes gave way on later trips only to more jumbled images. My first trip to Las Vegas—our first trip there together—was in August, 1990. Our second trip was in July, 1991.

I had begun to recognize by that time that the places we went to were going to be by and large clean, tidy, even pleasant. I had begun to recognize, too, that the food was going to be by and large good, sometimes very good, and reasonably priced. And I had begun to recognize that the systems along the Strip were by and large going to be efficient. Very little is allowed to stand in the way of gambling.

And I like to gamble. I'm not sure that I'd known that before, but by our second trip, I knew that I was probably always going to be ready to go to Las Vegas. I was made for Las Vegas. I think I am mostly undeceived by the efficient systems, mostly undeceived by the well-publicized claims of returns on gambling money, mostly undeceived by the careful designs that direct me to gambling areas and that keep me reasonably comfortable there. Mostly undeceived, I think, and yet I still believe. I believe a fortune is waiting. The next pull of the lever, the next spin of the wheel will bring it. I believe. Some possibility exists that I might in fact sell the family farm in order to gamble some more.

But I'm generally saved from recklessness. Before I went to

Las Vegas the first time, I had lived sixty years; most of that time, I lived more or less rationally, and that helped. For sixty years, all the way from West Texas, I had expected to be poor, even if I wasn't always, and that helped. A censor was born the same day I was in West Texas, a dark god who always whispered, "You must marshal what you have; you must earn what you get." That was a significant stay against recklessness. What had become in those sixty years a deep, nonrational fear also held me, a fear of being stranded, of being unable to get home. You've got to get home, even when you can't. And she knew how to quiet recklessness.

During that second trip in July, 1991, I discovered something else that makes Las Vegas appealing. Given what I understand of my own character otherwise, it was an odd discovery. In the ordinary course of my ordinary life, I want notice and attention. I hunger for stardom. I want to outlast time. I want to be seen. I crave visibility. In Las Vegas, I'm happy to disappear. I shouldn't have been surprised to learn that it was possible. In *A World of Strangers: Order and Action in Urban Public Space*, Lyn H. Lofland remarks that "To live in a city is, among many other things, to live surrounded by large numbers of persons whom one does not know. To experience the city is, among other things, to experience anonymity." As David Lowenthal suggests, once we are there, we are part of the Las Vegas milieu, but we never know *that* we are seen or *how* we are seen. Anonymity is restful for some given period of time, though it would be intolerable if it lasted. Invisibility is restful for a while. Relaxation from the tension twisted into the soul by the yearning for visibility is restful, even among crowds. In the crowds of Las Vegas, I can for a little while be free from responsibility. No one can find me to blame me or shame me for my sins, whether of omission or of commission. Of course the place is gaudy, garish, artificial, and greedy, but we watch, encapsulated, and feed for a little while the hungers of a different imagination. I have no wish to know the details of "reality" here, not what goes on backstage, not who really runs the place. In West Texas, I can't escape history and grief. In Las Vegas, we are always in the present. We are at ease, anonymous, isolated, alone, and for a little while, I love it.

I had begun, I thought, to understand this much. Then, after the second trip and before the third trip, I realized that Las Vegas had become important. It was a place.

Las Vegas had become a place, and we longed to go there. During the cold, dreary, dark days of December, 1991, and January, 1992, we said to each other, "If we can just make it to Las Vegas, then we'll be all right."

Many others have worked as hard, and many others have faced more grievous and immediate peril, but in those days we were bonetired and weary in our heads and maybe a little scared.

On Halloween, 1991, a drizzly day, she had slipped and fallen on our wet porch. Her leg broke just above the ankle. Some weeks later, an assortment of doctors diagnosed disorder in my belly, and one of them did surgery upon my person in mid-December. Another told me that I was to commence a yearlong program of chemotherapy near the end of January, 1992. We would start, he told me, with a fiveday sequence of heavy infusions—"frontloading," he called it—and then there would be a brief interval before we would begin the regular weekly program of infusions and pills.

We aimed at that interval. That's when we would go—if she was out of her cast, if I was able to get around. "If we can just make it to Las Vegas," we said to each other, "then we'll be all right."

Las Vegas had become a place in our minds, perhaps just a dreamscape we had imagined, perhaps a refuge we had created out of fond hopes. We knew it wasn't Eden, but perhaps it would be a haven where we'd be safe for a little while, out on the other side of darkness. We went in the interval, in February, 1992.

We would, of course, go again: in July, 1992, for a short visit worked in around the chemotherapy schedule; in March, 1993, for a celebration after chemotherapy was over and the doctor had taken me as evidence that he was a good doctor; in July, 1993; in January, 1994; and in May, 1994. I expect we'll go again, to the peculiar haven in the west.

Except that I haven't accounted for everything. I like gambling, but not just anywhere. I've tried it briefly in some of the new casinos that have recently been established on the Gulf Coast. I didn't like that at all. We had a small fling in a casino in Vienna, but I was uncomfortable there. I like the anonymity, but in some places anonymity is intolerable. I needed a haven. We both did. But you can't find a haven just any old place. Gambling has to be in the right place. Anonymity has to be in the right place. A haven can only be in the right place. I haven't yet entirely told how Las Vegas came to be the right place. I may yet.

As I expect most people do, we began early in our trips to fall into certain habits and progressions, partly by chance, partly because Las Vegas knows how to direct us one way, then pull us another. Except for one trip when we stayed at the Flamingo Hilton, we've always stayed at Bally's. We don't go to Las Vegas for the shows; we've seen a couple and enjoyed them, but we go to gamble. We don't go to Las Vegas to eat, but we soon also fell into particular habits and progressions for eating. We've depended on the coffee shop in Bally's mostly for breakfasts and late-night snacks. We like to have lunch at least once in Lindy's Deli at the Flamingo, and we usually have at least one meal at the Caribe Café in the Mirage. Once during each trip, at lunch, we go to the buffet in the Mirage for a food orgy, and we usually have dinner once in the Peking Market at the Flamingo. I was a little slow to realize, until she coached me along nicely and gently, that meals didn't have to be major events, that we didn't need or even want to take time away from gambling.

I was also a little slow to recognize that I became a little disgruntled—mildly grumpy, you might say—if we didn't stop in at the usual places.

And we did, before long, have our usual places, our habits

and progressions.

Our routes for gambling begin at Bally's. Our common-est route takes us next across the street to the Barbary Coast. Early on, I was enchanted by a bank of slot machines there, and ever since, we've stopped in to visit what we call "the little guys," after the figures that appear on the screen. Every once in a while, the machines play a little tinkly tune, and the figures change. The oranges become earth globes, the cherries become singers, the grapes transform to eggs with birds just hatching and chirping, and the bells turn into English gentle-men in pith helmets. During all of our trips I have faithfully contributed to their upkeep. In return, they have chirped and sung and smiled and played a tinkly little tune for my delight, but they have given me no money. There's also a roulette table in the Barbary Coast where we sometimes stop, but then we go on next door to the Flamingo. We play this and that there, but spend most of our time at a bank of quarter video poker machines in the new section at the back. On down the street, we sometimes stop in at Fitzgerald's, usually at Harrah's, and then we usually cross over the Strip to the Mirage. Often, we stay there a good while, often as not at a variety of machines, including a bank of quarter video poker machines, past the rain forest and on in the back comer near the buffet. When we've used up the Mirage, we go on to Caesar's Palace, then home to Bally's.

That is our commonest route. The next most common route is the other way around.

Now, since the new places have opened, there is a third. We take a bus to Excalibur, sometimes play there, sometimes not, then go to Luxor, which we've come to enjoy, then a walk across to the Tropicana, usually for a short visit, then across for a nice long stay at the MGM Grand.

When we're out at night, though of course we're wonderfully sophisticated people, we're enchanted by the lights by the great lion at the MGM Grand, by the powdered sugar castle that is Excalibur, by the glitter at the Barbary Coast, by the changing lights in the long stretch of the Strip outside Caesar's Palace and the Mirage, by the audacious long extravaganza at the Flamingo. Sometimes we stop and look awhile.

We have sometimes spent as much as twenty hours a day in the various casinos, though that includes an occasional moment for food. We don't go to Las Vegas for the shows, or for shopping, or for the swimming pools and spas, or for food. We go to gamble.

Our gambling, though extended in time, is limited in kind. Neither of us plays poker. I don't even go near the poker tables. Those people are serious, and they scare me. Neither of us plays at craps, though she's beginning to get pretty interested. I don't go near the tables. Those people are loud, and they scare me. We both enjoy roulette, though our playing time there is limited because we can't always find tables with chips that we can afford or minimum bets that we think we can handle. She loves blackjack and plays at the low-limits tables, but she doesn't allow me to play anymore. There have been a couple of near-ugly episodes involving me at blackjack tables: once when I believe I was taken to be irreverent about the protocols of the table, and once when I believe I was taken to be irreverent about the blackjack systems in practice on either side of me. She's concerned that I might get shot.

What that leaves is what is best, video poker and slot machines. We've spent hours at each, typically at quarter machines, though once on each trip we allow ourselves a modest splurge on some dollar machines. When we can find a nice bank of video poker machines and sit down in good clean places, when I can look down the way and watch her address her machine, discuss matters with it, then enter into the fairy world where she is queen, then all things are good and to my great content. Video poker machines weren't developed until the 1970s, and Bally Manufacturing, formed in 1931 to produce a pioneer pin game called Ballyhoo, didn't get into the market until 1983, though the company, I learn from Marshall Fey's *Slot Machines*, had virtually monopolized the Nevada market for slot machines since the 1960s. Fey reports that video poker was a great sensation by 1990. It certainly was with me. In video poker, I expect my fortune to accumulate.

At the slot machine, I expect it to come with the next pull.

Someone else might very well see my attitudes and actions in a different way, but I believe I am customarily moderate in most respects. But not always. Sometimes I am childish when I see others winning, resentful and pouty, altogether unkind and disagreeable. Clearly, I sometimes think to myself, those other people haven't earned their luck. But I have—by now I'm figuratively stomping my feet in a tantrum—I've worked hard. Why don't I win? I remember my first outing on our first trip. I had never played at slot machines before. I bought fifty dollars worth of dollar tokens, found a pretty machine—the machine has to be pretty—and sat down before it. I was ready. I would accept my fortune. I put in the fifty slugs, three at a time—and nothing came back. I lost it all. I still remember how sick I felt, and more, shocked. I hadn't won.

Mostly, though, I eventually remember to be sensible, even to be an adult. Mostly, I am moderate. We both are. Mostly, we stay sort of even. Mostly, we leave with just about as much money as we had when we came.

Sometimes, we win a little. During our trip in March, 1993, a quarter slot machine gave me 500 quarters on one pull, and another gave 300 quarters. I was pretty silly both times. Then, as we were leaving Bally's for the airport to return home, we put five dollars in a dollar video poker machine and drew four queens. That gave us $125, and I was silly and excited again. During our January, 1994, trip, playing together again, we put some dollar slugs in a slot machine at the MGM Grand, and it produced $300. I giggled a lot over that, and danced a little jig.

Sometimes, we lose, though not all that much. Still, it's shocking. Once in the airport as we were about to leave for home, she said, "You know, coming to Las Vegas and losing is like having a baby—it hurts so much you almost forget how much fun you had getting there."

But even when we lose, I keep three dollar slugs from Bally's back. It's a habit—silly enough, but mine—I developed early on. I keep them and carry them home with me, and then when we go back, we play them. Over sort of in the back of Bally's, not far from the lounge, there is a dollar slot machine with a dumb cartoon baseball player on its face. I'm devoted to that machine. That's where we play the three dollars. It has not, so far, been devoted to me. But whatever happens, I keep three dollar-slugs back for the next time. They're in my pocket now.

Most of the time, though, she doesn't lose much, if at all. Whenever she wins, even a small amount, she puts some or all of it away. She doesn't much like the idea of putting winnings back into a machine.

And most of the time, she knows how to keep me from losing too much. She comes to where I am and says, maybe, "Can I come play with you?" or maybe, "Do you want to come play with me?" When she says something like that in a private place, I get pretty excited, but I don't faint. When she says it in public in Las Vegas, she has reckoned that I'm on the edge of hocking my watch and her jewelry and throwing in the car and the house just for another round of chances at a pretty machine. She has reckoned that I'm ready for a little quiet. And so we play together, sitting together at a machine, taking turns dropping the coins in, taking turns at pulling some lever or pressing some button, and everything is all right.

Slowly, I've learned from her about playing in Las Vegas.

Gambling is fun. I love to gamble. But the trick is to be able to keep on gambling. The point is to play, I learn from her, and to keep on playing, to take a little time out from that other world, to plunge into this world of life and color and movement and silly life, and to play and to keep on playing. I was a little slow to learn that, but sometimes I forget, and then she'll say, "Can I come play with you?"

In *The Feast of Fools*, Harvey Cox inquires, "Why did the virtues of sobriety, thrift, industry, and ambition gain such prominence at the expense of other values? Why did mirth, play, and festivity come in for such scathing criticism during the Protestant era?" I should say two things right away in reply. First, I don't know the answers to Cox's questions. I have lived and worked in the world adumbrated in his questions, lived and worked more than thought that world, finding that world inescapable. I have not even been devoted to work, for that suggests choice: I have simply worked, though I have not thereby purchased prosperity. Second, I don't believe that I have been publicly scathing in criticism of mirth, play, festivity, but I have been privately dubious, sometimes condescending, occasionally condemnatory, wondering if they don't end, as Cox supposes they might, in vacuous frivolity. Though such things should be found out by others rather than proclaimed by oneself, though my wisdom in saying so must rest not on what I say, but on how I am seen, I am the pure embodiment of the Protestant work ethic, and therefore imperfect. Some forms of what Cox calls "noninstrumental significance" are familiar to me, and I know that it is sweet and good to sit at the roadside rest area north of Jayton and look down and out into Putoff Canyon into the blue that lies yonder, for no purpose except to sit and to look, and I know that it is sweet and good to linger on, under, and beside her. But play has been harder to reach.

Play, Huizenga says, "is a thing by itself," but civilization "has grown more serious," assigning "only a secondary place to playing." Huizenga's definition of play—"a voluntary activity or occupation executed within certain fixed limits of time and place, according to rules freely accepted but absolutely binding, having its aim in itself and accompanied by a feeling of tension, joy and the consciousness that it is 'different' from 'ordinary life'" —attaches a minor significance to place, echoed in his suggestion that play and ritual are identical, the "hallowed spot" of ritual originally having been a playground, but his later discussions don't appear to carry much concern otherwise for place:

> It has not been difficult to show that a certain play-factor was extremely active all through the cultural process and that it produces many of the fundamental forms of social life. The spirit of playful competition is, as a social impulse, older than culture itself and pervades all life like a veritable ferment. Ritual grew up in sacred play; poetry was born in play and nourished on play; music and danc-

ing were pure play. Wisdom and philosophy
found expression in words and forms derived
from religious contests. The rules of warfare,
the conventions of noble living were built
up on play-patterns. We have to conclude,
therefore, that civilization is, in its earliest
phases, played. It does not come from play
like a babe detaching itself from the womb: it
arises in and as play, and never leaves it.

I don't know much about civilization. I have believed that I
arise in and as work. Mostly I haven't worked hard enough.

If I like to imagine that I am identified with work, that may
even be encouraging to play. In his book *In Tune With the World*,
Josef Pieper proposes that "a festival can arise only out of the
foundation of a life whose ordinary shape is given by the working day." Otherwise, Pieper doesn't help me much. His subject
is festival, not play. Festival has meaning it itself, he says, while
play does not: "Human acts derive their meaning primarily
from their content, from their object, not from the manner in
which they are performed. Play, however, seems to be chiefly a
mere modus of action, a specific way of performing something,
at any rate a purely formal determinant."

I don't much think Las Vegas is a hallowed spot or the scene
of celebratory festival, but I have found blessings there. "I know
nothing, except what everyone knows," Auden says, "if there

when Grace dances, I should dance."

There is a there there. I begin to think that play, for me, is situated, placed.

Victor Turner's introduction to *Celebration*, though chiefly concerned with public festivity and ritual, opens other possibilities. Ease comes with play, though not easily, and play is in one way or another placed. I begin to learn that you don't have to become a child again to play. I begin to learn that play may be public, though it doesn't have to be, and that you can play privately, even in public. I learn, too, that what Turner calls the vivacity and what Durkheim called the effervescence generated by groups of people in celebration she can generate by herself. The words and games and material objects—the image clusters of play in Las Vegas—may, as Turner suggests, be "refractory to standardized verbal interpretation," though I keep trying. In the celebratory process, Turner says,

> . . . we cannot detach the participants from what they participate in, the subject from the object. From the subject's sensorium, his "withinside," such clusters are no longer experienced as detached from him, held at arm's length, merely cognized. They invade him, alter his mode of perceiving, daze or dazzle him. He is made vulnerable to imprintment by whatever message is being conveyed by the symbolic cluster. In celebration, private

> space is thus socialized, encultured; social
> space is correspondingly made private.

Such vivacity as we may enjoy may, I know, not be subject to interpretation by others, for it will depend upon the stress, intensity, energy, and focus we have previously given to work and now give to play. In her paper, "Too Many, Too Few: Ritual Modes of Signification," Barbara Babcock suggests that "a surplus of signifiers"—in our instance, the image clusters, words, sounds, sights of Las Vegas— "creates a selftransgressive discourse which mocks and subverts the monological arrogance of 'official' systems of signification." What she calls "carnivalesque discourse" is a statement "in praise and a demonstration of the creative potential of human signification as opposed to its instrumental and representative use."

Much of our play in Las Vegas is our ritual. We play here, then we play there, and then we play yonder. In each place, we play this, then we play that, and then we play the other. Our ritual doesn't qualify as ritual by some standards. In "The Contemporary Ritual Milieu," Frederick Bird defines rituals as "culturally transmitted symbolic codes which are stylized, regularly repeated, dramatically structured, authoritatively designated and intrinsically valued." The symbolic codes of Las Vegas are already there when we arrive and are in that sense transmitted to us. Our ritual is stylized and, for us, dramatically structured. Our ritual is, for us, intrinsically valued. But it is not authoritatively designated. It might be argued, I suppose, that our ritual is, after all, authoritatively designated in the sense that we play what Las Vegas allows and encourages us to play. But then, we are free not to play much of what Las Vegas allows and encourages us to play.

Others, however, might allow ours as ritual. Not all rituals arise in ancient, unknowable settings. In "Myths and Rituals: A General Theory," Clyde Kluckhohn remarks that "there are a number of well documented actual cases where historical persons, in the memory of other historical persons, actually instituted new rituals." He cites the "American Indian Ghost Dance cult" as an example. Later, he says,

> There are always individuals in every society who have their private rituals; there are always individuals who dream and have compensatory phantasies. In the normal course of things these are simply deviant behaviors which are ridiculed or ignored by most members of the society. Perhaps indeed one should not speak of them as "deviant"—they are "deviant" only as carried to extremes by a relatively small number of individuals, for everyone probably has some private rituals and compensatory phantasies.

Deviant or not, we have our ritual. A ritual helps to make a place, but first, I think, a ritual has to have a place.

What makes a place a place? When does a place become a place? How do you know when you get there?

I don't belong in Las Vegas any more than I belong in West Texas.

I do belong in the West Texas of my mind and in the Las Vegas of my mind.

I don't love Las Vegas, but I am eager to be there. It is a place, and I like to be there.

The ideological content of my encounters with Las Vegas is, I believe, pretty skimpy and generally unsurprising. I don't go to Las Vegas because I fancy myself a cowboy gambler. I did believe that I wanted to be a cowboy for about a month when I was eight, but it didn't last. I do go to Las Vegas expecting to win my fortune. I do probably carry with me to Las Vegas residual thoughts from old time telling me that if I'm going to sin, and enjoy sinning, I'd better do it elsewhere, not at home. And I do carry around all of the time another loony leftover from who knows what accumulation of stories, books, movies, radio programs. Except for small trails into the interior, I have never imagined myself an explorer or a settler in new territory, but when I come to country that I like—say the White Mountains in New Hampshire or the Croton Breaks in West Texas or the rough country across northern Arizona and on up to Las Vegas—I always try to imagine what it would be like to be an explorer or a settler seeing it for the first time. The foolish hope I've had, time and again, of walking and earning my way to the Double Mountains or to Las Vegas or to elsewhere is another form of the same dreaming, that if I walked and earned my way, then I'd be an explorer or settler seeing country for the first time, really seeing it, really knowing. Then, perhaps, I could claim it as my own.

Slowly, I learn how Las Vegas began to become a place for me. The Strip is a fine place to gamble; I like to gamble. Even in the noise and movement of the casinos, it's possible to be quietly anonymous, and I like that. Perhaps it became a haven where I didn't have to think hard thoughts. The play I watched and learned there is exhilarating, and I like that.

But all of that together will not quite account for what happened between me and Las Vegas. I know the risks and limits of gambling. I don't at all like anonymity elsewhere. Havens are seldom real or permanent. I have played elsewhere, though not often so dramatically.

Something else had to happen.

Gambling and anonymity and haven and play, for me, have to be placed, in the right place. The place has to be a place you can claim. You have to be able to stake your claim.

Slowly through the course of our trips to Las Vegas, I began to remember what was already in my mind and to notice what was accumulating there.

I began to understand a little more clearly when I discovered one day that I was pouting about Bally's. Bally's was the first place we stayed in Las Vegas. She was making arrangements for our next trip, and it had begun to look as if we'd not be able to get reservations at Bally's. That's when I commenced to pout, then graduated up to surliness. I realized, then, that Bally's was not just the first place we stayed in Las Vegas—in my mind, it apparently had become the only place to stay in Las Vegas.

In any area of human interest and enterprise, the first lessons we learn are powerful, far more powerful, I think, than we regularly recognize and acknowledge. Sometimes, we cannot shed them even if we should, even if we want to rid ourselves of them. I cannot free myself of the first lessons I learned, or have imagined that I learned. Sometimes I attribute those lessons to my mother and father, but perhaps they didn't teach them all: some of them I think I breathed in with the gloomy Calvinistic air of depression and Dust Bowl times in West Texas. No matter what philosophical and theological enlightenment comes my way, I still know that I will go to the Hell the preacher told about, made of fire and regret. I have from time to time used a fountain pen, a manual typewriter, an electric typewriter, and a word processor, but despite all advances, I still believe that if you're going to do real writing, you use a fountain pen. The first lessons some children learn are gang lessons. The first lessons some learn are xenophobic. The first lessons some learn are lessons of poverty, violence, and neglect. Sometimes, the first lessons are so powerful and pervasive that we never learn what they are, can never learn otherwise.

The first place you come to and know has power to situate and to determine ensuing thought and behavior. Bally's was the first place for me; very quickly, it became the only place. Maslow's experiments, as Harvey Cox recounts them,

> ... seem to indicate the normal functioning of
> personality depends on the subject's halfcon-
> scious awareness of a background of sensory
> items of orientation. Ordinarily, a person is
> not aware of this background, but when it is
> taken away or markedly altered, his percep-
> tion of reality is dangerously undermined.

YiFu Tuan remarks that "paradoxes abound" in our reactions
to places. We can be at home in a place, emplaced, for example,
but if we think about our place, we are distanced and separated
from it, displaced. I was, or so I regarded myself, absolutely
an alien in Las Vegas. Once there, once in an environment
long enough for it to become familiar to me, I left off thinking
about it, and was emplaced, in place at Bally's.

Then I could look outward and go outward on what would
become our familiar routes. Anne Buttimer says that "most
life forms need a *home* and *horizons of reach* outward from that
home." These "horizons of reach" became so important to me,
she contends, that if I'm led the wrong way, or miss one of the
stations on our routes, I'm inclined to bawl like Benjy, driven
the wrong way around the square in *The Sound and the Fury*.
I'm not entirely idiosyncratic in such behavior. Randy Hester
tells how he and citizens of Manteo, North Carolina, set out
to find the valued places in the community before initiating a
plan for community revitalization. "Life style and landscape

were intertwined," they found, and "Daily ritual had place specificity . . . " From questionnaires, observation, and close registration of the time, frequency, and regularity of citizens' visits to various places in town, they discovered that the most valued places were not necessarily the "important" places, but were likelier to be the humbler places that were the settings for the community's daily routines—what Hester calls "sub-conscious landscapes of the heart." We had found, or created, such places ourselves.

Eventually, I began to pay attention to what else was happening in my mind, to the words and pictures jumbled there. I set out with her for Las Vegas the first time in considerable trepidation. Once there, I knew I had come to a wilderness. I preferred home. I preferred mesquite trees and cactus and sagebrush and quiet and space. I had come to a wilderness. In *Wilderness and the American Mind*, Roderick Nash says that "Any place in which a person feels stripped of guidance, lost, and perplexed may be called a wilderness." I finally realized that I was thinking of Las Vegas as a wilderness and calling it a wilderness. She uses the city far more easily and happily than I am so far able to do; she doesn't want to miss any of it. I have been slow to learn such gladness, though I take delight in her instruction.

I had been thinking of Las Vegas as a wilderness and calling it a wilderness in my mind. But we stayed a while at Bally's, and it began to seem a little familiar. By and by, I realized that I was thinking of Bally's as the home place, the clearing we had made in the wilderness. Our daily routes—what I have called our rituals, though another would think them only our Las Vegas habits—helped by bringing us back each night to the clearing we had made, and I began to see that we had staked our claim. Our daily paths out into the wilderness gradually became a little more comfortable: we found a spring here, a little meadow yonder, a gentle plain and a low hill farther along, a green bower down the way, and we returned at night to the claim we had staked. One day, we'd have a cabin there.

When I look back now, I see that I had, after all, become an explorer and a settler in my mind.

But I didn't see it all and know it all and earn it all. I created it. I built Las Vegas out of a wilderness, converting it to my terms, omitting most of the place from my consideration, turning happily, and returning, to the clearing and the paths I imagined we had made.

I am responsible for Las Vegas. A biography of landscapes, Merwyn Samuels says in "The Biography of Landscape," is "not everywhere or always feasible."

> Countless millions of faceless and nameless peasants and townsfolk the world over have through the centuries molded, designed, and designated their environments in the form of land use patterns and monuments to state grandeur without having left so much as an "X" for a signature. Having dis-

appeared into the landscape much as their corporeal selves have turned to dust in some forgotten stretch of a Great Wall or ancient fendike, we can barely hope to ever recover the datum of their persona. Like archaeologists left with only the artifacts of man, social scientists and historians alike are often limited to speculation, inference, and an intuitive feel about the making and meaning of human landscapes.

I don't know Las Vegas, but I have created Las Vegas: I do not escape the particularities of myself. My will is suspect, my senses are unreliable, my judgment is idiosyncratic, I am constrained by chemistry and molecule imprints, but I am not irrelevant. Every individual, Samuel proposes, constitutes an elite who molds and gives meaning to an environment by virtue of choice. To be sure, the implementation of choice is often limited to those who, for one reason or another, have the means to overcome or escape social, economic, political, legal, educational, physical, or other constraints. Indirectly, the geography of socioeconomic indicators is undeniably a geography of those with greater or lesser means to effect choice. But even in the most socially limiting circumstances of birth, race, wealth, education, or position, individuals ceaselessly emerge to mold and create their own landscapes. The signposts of individual expression are hardly hidden for those who care to look. They are there in the literature, art, dance, and theater of the "folk," the poor, and the "masses." They are evident in the vernacular poetry, graffiti, and media of the ghetto. They are there in the dramatic and notsodramatic *persona* of the Lower East Side, Harlem, and Watts. They are there, too, in village elders, clan spokesmen, and in story tellers. They are, in short, almost everywhere.

I, for example, am over here, and I have made Las Vegas, building it, as MerleauPonty might have put it, from the lumber found in partial space.

Las Vegas became a place when I had created it in my mind, with a home place in a safe clearing, with paths that will let me go out and come back. "The surface of the earth," David Lowenthal says, "is shaped for each person by refraction through cultural and personal lenses of custom and fancy. We are all artists and landscape architects, creating order and organizing space, time, and causality in accordance with our apperceptions and predilections." Las Vegas is there in what we have agreed to call Nevada, east of Los Angeles, west of West Texas. Las Vegas is also where I created it, out yonder. Las Vegas is not half one, half the other. Each is entire, and the Las Vegas of my mind and the Las Vegas of reality are equally subjective and objective.

I don't believe that I have confused fact and fantasy, as Ada Louise Huxtable suggests in a discussion of Williamsburg, Disneyland, theme parks, and various versions of doctored reality. I don't believe I have merely sanitized Las Vegas by selection. I don't want to "ignore the actual deposits of history and humanity that make our cities vehicles of a special kind of art and experience, gritty accumulations of the best and worst we have produced." Neither do I want to ignore my own creation. I reckon that you have to get in a place in some way that will let you think. Many of our ways of doing that are as inadequate as mine, and some are worse. I reckon that we ought to learn new ways of thinking, though it's beginning to look as if I probably won't. I am lonesome for the Las Vegas that I do not know and will not know, and I remember that, as Lowenthal puts it, "every marvel unattained is a Paradise Lost." Every artifact of the city is compelling; every artifact is also only a pale reflection of what Lowenthal calls "the lapidary architecture of the mind." I am lonesome for the Las Vegas that I do not know, and I am eager to see the Las Vegas that I made.

I made it the jackleg way, the only carpentry I can manage, with a few new boards, a bunch of warped boards from the past, some baling wire, and a few rusty nails. It isn't much. I hope it will hold until I learn better.

She does it better. She's open to the city. She's easy with the city. She faces the city. And she uses it up. At home, she rummages weekly among garage sales, flea markets, and antique malls and brings back treasures. She uses the treasures to make the house into a kind of continuing art work, what she calls a three-dimensional collage. She uses everything, sorting and choosing, placing and putting, and. doing it all again until she's content, and then she'll do it again and be content in a new way.

I've not learned yet to use the world so well. When I set out to build Las Vegas, I missed some things and dismissed others and forgot others. The city I made tilts a little. A hard wind down out of the northwest might blow it over.

Afterword
James S. Baumlin and Keith D. Miller

A previous collection (*Selected Essays of Jim W. Corder: Pursuing the Personal in Scholarship, Teaching, and Writing*) highlighted Corder's contributions to rhetorical theory and pedagogy. This present volume puts to practice many of the precepts that his more scholarly writing theorizes; at the same time, it highlights the man's literary personality, giving free rein to the *ethos* expressed elsewhere, albeit in more muted tones. From that earlier collection, one might come to know Corder's ways of theorizing; but there's still more of him left over, and the theorist and belletrist need to be kept in close touch, allowing each if not to complete, then at least to soften and ironize and complicate the other.

Corder himself suggests as much in his playfully anti-academic, personal-scholarly essay, "Tribes and Displaced Persons":

> I haven't yet learned how to be myself. . . .
> I don't want to learn how to be someone
> else. I can't be Maynard Mack, whose work
> I admired so much when I was in graduate
> school, and I probably won't turn out to
> be Jacques Derrida. I want to try to think
> my thoughts, which aren't altogether mine.
> I don't want to write in the languages of
> the academic communities I have almost

belonged to for years. . . . I want to do a scholarly sort of work but to write in a personal sort of way. . . . I want to write in my way, . . . and perhaps even stretch out the possibilities of prose.

Corder played the academic game well enough, passing through the *cursus honorum* of professor to department head, college dean, and vice chancellor at Texas Christian University. Yet he often expressed diffidence in the academic priesthood, avowing to hide from his students "how little" he knew. He was never satisfied with his labor, always looking to be more (or, at least, elsewhere) intellectually and artistically. The fact that Corder worked in so many forms, seeking to "stretch out the possibilities of prose," reflects his intellectual and artistic restlessness, as well as his need to harness the nervous/creative energies that spilled over and into his memoirs.

An aim of this present collection, then, is to introduce Corder's appreciative readers to some new territory. He did, in fact, enjoy two distinct audiences, one academic, one belletristic; only his colleagues, students, and most devoted readers will be aware that Jim W. Corder, Professor of English at TCU and co-author of the best-selling *Handbook of Current English,* also authored *Yonder: Life on the Far Side of Change* and *Hunting Lieutenant Chadbourne,* among other works of personal remembrance and creative nonfiction. Professor Corder's readers will be surprised (and, we trust, delighted) to learn of his belletristic side; readers of Corder the personal essayist will not be surprised, but will find themselves in new places still, as this collection gathers together works lesser known or previously unpublished.

In light moments, Corder spoke wistfully of a wish to be acclaimed a minor poet. Whereas poetry is the least practiced of his literary genres, he remained a voracious reader and critic of contemporary verse, stocking his personal library with scores of chapbooks. In "When (Do I/Shall I/May I/Must I/Is It Appropriate for Me to) (Say No to/Deny/Resist/Repudiate/Attack/Alter) Any (Poem/Poet/Other Piece of the World) for My Sake?"—an essay on the ethics of reading and response—Corder reminds us that criticism is "inevitable, inherent, desirable." As he writes,

> The examined life, one of our great aims, is a life of criticism. We need criticism, have a right to criticism, enjoy great hopes for criticism, and exercise it diversely. By criticism we come to know ourselves, to speak for ourselves, to make our intentions known to others, to claim the works of others for ourselves. Criticism is inevitable, inherent, desirable; it is necessary to the free citizen.
>
> Criticism is also a peril to all save the critic. It is a displacement of others by the self, a replacement of others with the self. Even the

> most unquestionably benevolent criticism is
> potent with peril for others. Unmaking oth-
> ers, we make ourselves. . . .

Thus he guides readers toward benevolent criticism of his own work, acknowledging at the same time the author's need to move aside, making room for the reader's response. Since Corder did not always keep copies, his poems remain rare finds, scattered about in mostly small, regional journals. The example we include—on the passing of a famous if flawed sports figure—fits the thematics of this collection.

An accomplished amateur in pen and ink, Corder regularly illustrated his own prose. Though his hands sometimes shook while holding coffee or lighting his pipe, the pen seemed to steady his nerves, yielding some finely detailed line drawings. The art presented here reflects two twining themes: the fleeting images of popular culture (particularly of Hollywood cowboys and ball players) and the ghostly landscape of Depression-era West Texas.

Of course, it was not as a poet or artist, nor as a rhetorician or writing teacher, but as a practicing essayist that Corder sought himself and fashioned himself most intensely. Those readers who knew him personally will hear his living voice intoned throughout the pieces gathered here. They will hear the chesty though whispery speech, the slow, carefully shaped cadences (often classical, often Scriptural in their formal patterning), the scholarly diction intermixed with the colloquial, all brought into harmony by a West Texas accent. Those who knew him cannot help but hear him in the prose. While reading (as Roland Barthes suggests) demands the "death of the author," reading can also be a necromancy, a raising of the once-living voice that continues, in some real if indeterminable sense, to resound in the writing. Of course those new to his writing will need, as Corder would say, to hunt the author down, bearing witness to his *ethos*.

That hunt begins in West Texas. Corder's many scattered autobiographical writings attest that his blue-collar family struggled to outlast the Great Depression, which hammered everyone in and around Jayton, "a town of 700 souls," as he describes it. At age ten, Corder moved with his family from rural Jayton to Fort Worth, an unimaginably large city, where steady work beckoned his father. He later attended TCU, where he would return to teach after a stint in the army (drafted, he served with the American occupation forces in Mannheim, Germany) and doctoral study at the University of Oklahoma.

The persona Corder creates in these works left Jayton, and yet never left. Again and again—in and throughout this collection—Corder revisits his childhood, wherein fundamentalist church services, racy comic books, local sports pages, and radio broadcasts (particularly of football games from then-distant Fort Worth) fired a young boy's imagination, shaping his beliefs and aspirations while linking him to the world beyond his otherwise self-enclosed community.

For Corder, moving into the university meant escaping from

manual labor, financial hardship, and brimstone Protestant-
ism into a life of teaching, bookishness, and religious toler-
ance. While his considerable writerly achievements earned
him a national reputation, they also alienated him from that
early self-image, rooted firmly in Jayton. Though the doctor-
ate raised him out of geographical isolation, the pain of his
uprooting never diminished; nor, indeed, was the uprooting
ever complete. In his mature writings, Jayton remains both psy-
chologically distant and hauntingly present. The distance and
tension between town and gown helped structure the complex,
adult self.

The mature Corder's yearning to revisit old haunts, to remember his family and heal the wounds of uprooting, proved at
least as strong as his yearning for escape into academia. Com-
paratively meager educational and cultural opportunities did
not destroy the jaw-dropping wonder of childhood; and while
the task of recovering that wonder could not be completed, it
remained forever urgent.

Recovering the early years was, for Corder, never an entirely
nostalgic enterprise. Recovery of the openness and joy of
childhood entailed also a recovery *from* childhood—from its
deceptions and delusions. For Corder, one's difficult yet necessary task remains to reawaken the somnolent adult self from
smothering routine and incessant obligations; one must shed
the illusions fostered by one's early upbringing, even as one
expresses respect and love for the flawed adults responsible for
that upbringing.

Through it all, baseball provided a precious thread of continuity, linking child and adult versions of self. In a world otherwise marked by change and loss, baseball offered the promise of an eternal present, wherein everyone bats "and no one dies." As a child, Corder played baseball—of course. Eagerly, he read of Joe DiMaggio and Charlie Gehringer, whose feats in distant, mythic ballpark-cathedrals he would himself ritually, imaginatively reenact in his own Dust Bowl schoolyard. He stood marvelling when his older brother, a high-school athlete of modest talent, went off to war. DiMaggio, Ted Williams, and other of his baseball heroes left for war as well. In so doing, they identified the athlete with the soldier or pilot and confirmed the young Corder's belief in a Romantic, masculinist moral code, wherein athletic prowess and warrior manhood became mirror images and warfare, like sport, would be fought "by the rules," in gentlemanly manner.

Later, having been drafted and witnessing the effects of Allied saturation bombing, Corder questioned his childhood idealization of the male warrior-athlete; he would not, however, forget baseball and its promise of individual heroic action. He searched for new heroes to replace DiMaggio and Gehringer. As a graduate student, when tired of reading Maynard Mack, he practiced pitching. As a middle-aged professor, he joined softball teams. He tracked the career of Mickey Mantle, who succeeded DiMaggio in centerfield and (despite his alcoholism) achieved an equally fabled place in the lineup of Yankee mythology. As a father, Corder marvelled at his son's pitching victories, which included two no-hitters. For him, it seemed possible to retrieve baseball as an innocent, purely sportive pursuit; for, despite the examples of DiMaggio and Williams, baseball did not require athletes to go to war.

As Yi-Fu Tuan has argued, geography shapes cosmology, contributing to cultural formation and self-formation. For Corder as for Tuan, the human creature remains an incurable topophiliac. And Corder-the-scholar fully supported the belletrist's fascination with self-making and one's home-places. As he would teach students, all writing remains personal at its expressive core, the word "I" lurking within every utterance, however dry or apparently impersonal, appealing to the Other for a witness and, if possible, for assent. Through the last two decades of an academic career that spanned from the 1950s to the late 1990s, Corder's writing—regardless of genre, topic, or audience, and despite his intense engagement with postmodernist theory—remained a continuous personal essay.

Since his passing in 1998, the profession of English has seen an explosion of interest and activity in the so-called "fourth genre" of creative nonfiction; had Corder lived to polish the several book-length manuscripts that he left behind, we suspect that he would be acknowledged a leading voice in this emergent genre. But these manuscripts—on sport and popular culture, on travel and the psychology of place (including *nostalgia* or one's mourning over lost place), on the multeity of rhetorics—remain imperfect: remnants and leftovers as it were, occasionally brilliant and always suggestive, typically a revision shy of completion.

The materials gathered here prove an exception. A chapter from the unpublished *Places in the Mind: Essays on Rhetorical Sites*, "Making Las Vegas" is a carefully researched, stylistically nuanced, topophiliac exploration of a specific city and of image-making in postmodern popular culture. Such work shows Corder at the height of his powers. We are also pleased to include *The Glove* in its near-entirety. (The title has been taken from its first chapter, the manuscript remaining otherwise unnamed.) Sections of two chapters that we have excised appear elsewhere in our collection: previously published, "The Rock-Kicking Championship of the Whole World" and "The Heroes Have Gone from the Grocery Store" speak, we believe, more strongly on their own. In separating these essays from the larger, later manuscript, we have left a few brief redundancies and inconsistencies unedited. (For example: "Rock-Kicking Championship" describes Jayton as a town of "700 souls," a figure that shrinks in *The Glove* to "about 650." Such is the mark of a twice-told tale.)

If a word might suffice to describe projects of his final years, it would be *tentative*: and paradoxically so, since Corder fought mightily against time to complete his life's work. The fact that his work remains forever in-progress, unsettled and apparently incompletable, remains a distinctively Corderian touch. In this respect, too, Corder's writing confirms postmodern notions of *bricolage*. In an essay that one of us was honored to co-author with him, Corder reflects upon qualities of the bricoleur's trade, known in West Texas as "jackleg carpentry":

> Jackleg carpentry (and one can practice any-
> thing, certainly writing, in the jackleg way)
> may be defined as that mode in which, upon
> completion of a job, the carpenter backs off,
> surveys the work, and says, "Well, there it is
> by God,—it ain't much, but it'll hold us until
> we can think of something better."

Out of such *bricolage* arises Corder's philosophy of writing, his
philosophy of living and of being-in-the-world:

> It seems that discourse must always be jack-
> legged. It must, for its own health, never
> be fixed, never perfect or complete, never,
> really, a product to be judged as complete or
> (worse) owned and sold. It must only (and
> always) be good enough, capable of change,
> always in motion. Discourse, when we think it
> is perfected (and perfection means comple-
> tion) is a dead thing to the writer, incapable
> of allowing growth. We must always, for this
> reason, jackleg our discourse, in the same way
> we jackleg so many other things in our lives.
> . . . Other things we can own, even admire;
> only the jacklegged things can be continually

present and involved in our being. . . . We may often have despaired of jackleg carpentry, yearning for the well-crafted, the finished, the definitive. We should have known better, or as well: there is no sadness in jackleg carpentry, only wonder.

So it is with the jackleggery of Corder's literary remains: there is no sadness . . . only wonder.

Works Cited

Baumlin, James S., and Keith D. Miller, eds. *Selected Essays of Jim W. Corder: Pursuing the Personal in Scholarship, Teaching, and Writing.* Foreword by Wendy Bishop. Urbana, IL: NCTE, 2004.

Baumlin, James S., and Jim W. Corder. "Jackleg Carpentry and the Fall from Freedom into Authority in Writing." *Freshman English News* 18 (1990): 18-25.

Corder, Jim W. *Chronicle of a Small Town.* College Station: Texas A&M UP, 1989.

_____. *The Glove.* Unpublished ms. 1998.

_____. *Hunting Lieutenant Chadbourne.* Athens, GA: U of Georgia P, 1993.

_____. *Lost in West Texas.* College Station, TX: Texas A&M UP, 1988.

_____. *Places in the Mind:* Essays on Rhetorical Sites. Unpublished ms. 1998.

_____. *Scrapbook.* Unpublished ms. 1998.

_____. "Tribes and Displaced Persons: Some Observations on Collaboration." *Theory and Practice in the Teaching of Writing: Rethinking the Discipline.* Ed. Lee Odell. Carbondale: Southern Illinois UP, 1993. 271-288.

_____. "When (Do I/Shall I/May I/Must I/Is It Appropriate for Me to) (Say No to/Deny/Resist/Repudiate/Attack/ Alter) Any Poem/Poet/Other Piece of the World) for My Sake?" *Rhetoric Society Quarterly* 13 (1988): 49-68.

_____. *Yonder: Life on the Far Side of Change.* Athens: U of Georgia

P, 1992.

Corder, Jim W., and John Ruszkiewicz. *Handbook of Current English*. 8th ed. (Glenview, IL: Scott, Foresman, 1989.

Tuan, Yi-Fu. *Topophilia: A Study of Environmental Perception, Attitudes, and Values*. 1974. New York: Columbia UP, 1990.

Acknowledgments

We thank Roberta Corder for permission to print Jim W. Corder's artwork, "Making Las Vegas," and *The Glove*. Several works reprinted here originally appeared in *Arete: The Journal of Sports Literature*, later renamed *Aethlon*: "The Rock-Kicking Championship of the Whole World, Now and Forevermore" (4 [1987]: 1-6), "The Heroes Have Gone From the Grocery Store" (5 [1987]: 73-78), and "Mickey Mantle, August 10, 1995" (12 [1995]: 44). "World War II on Cleckler Street" first appeared in *Collective Heart: Texans in World War II*, ed. Joyce Gibson Roach (Austin: Eakin, 1996 [18-28]). We thank the editors of *Arete/Aethlon* and Eakin Press for permission to reprint these materials.

We also thank Jason Christian for his design work, Casey D. White for his diligent proofing of the manuscript (errors remaining fall to us), and Craig A. Meyer for adding the finishing touches

CPSIA information can be obtained at www.ICGtesting.com
Printed in the USA
LVOW130917100113

315140LV00001B/5/P